STUDENTS' PREFACE

As you turn the pages of this book,
We ask you, "Take a closer look."
When you look deep inside,
You'll find a friend who seems to hide.
They may not be able to sing or dance,
But everyone deserves a chance.
When you see someone who's not the same,
Ask that person to join the game.
The game of life, we're talking about.
You'll learn the most leaving no one out.

This book was written from a kid's point of view. We have been inspired by the people we wrote about. They have not let anything stop them from living a good life. These students have come forward with their dreams and shared their courage.

We, the 245 authors, are students in the third through sixth grades. With the help of 16 teachers, we have produced *Kids Explore the Gifts of Children with Special Needs*. We hope you will learn as much from reading about these neat people as we have learned from writing about them.

KIDS EXPLORE THE GIFTS OF CHILDREN WITH SPECIAL NEEDS

Westridge Young Writers Workshop

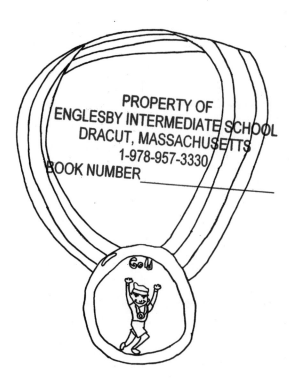

John Muir Publications
Santa Fe, New Mexico

When you read this book you will learn
All kinds of people make the world turn.
Each is different in his or her own way,
We want you to know that that's okay.
These heroes have taught us things we didn't know,
Now along with us you can grow.

This book is dedicated to each of our new friends, who shared their dreams
and inspired us to be the best we can be.

John Muir Publications, P.O. Box 613, Santa Fe, NM 87504
© 1994 by Jefferson County School District N. R-1
Cover © 1994 John Muir Publications
All rights reserved. Published 1994
Printed in the United States of America

First edition. Third printing August 1994
          First TWG printing January 1994

Library of Congress Cataloging-in-Publication Data
Kids explore the gifts of children with special needs / by Westridge Young Writers Workshop.
  p.   cm.
ISBN 1-56261-156-9
1. Handicapped children—Education—United States—Juvenile literature. 2. Handicapped children—
United States—Biography—Juvenile literature. I. Westridge Young Writers Workshop.
LC4031.K46 1994
371.91—dc20   93-25922
                                                                  CIP
                                                                  AC

Cover art: Tony D'Agostino
Design: Susan Surprise
Typefaces: Garamond and Helvetica
Typography: Ken Wilson
Printer: Malloy Lithographing

Distributed to the book trade by   Distributed to the education market by
W. W. Norton & Co., Inc.   Wright Group Publishing, Inc.
500 Fifth Avenue   19201 120th Avenue NE
New York, NY 10110   Bothell, WA 98011

Photos © Anthony Allen, Mark Dickson, Diane Holstein, Christie Logsdon, Lori Stober, and John Twohig

CONTENTS

ACKNOWLEDGMENTS

We, the 245 authors, are very grateful to the ten young people featured in this book. We thank them for sharing their inspiring stories with us and their families for helping us. We would also like to thank the many experts and volunteers who came to talk to us and helped us understand more about different disabilities and medical problems. We want to thank all of the schools and individuals who helped us locate the courageous young stars in this book. A special thanks goes to the volunteer readers who took part in the project and checked our writing for sensitivity and accuracy. Many thanks also go to the Jefferson Foundation and First Bank of South Jeffco for providing financial help. Last but not least, we thank the students and staff of all the schools that took part in the project, including Bromwell Elementary, Cherokee Trail Elementary, Children's Hospital Medical Day Treatment School, Deane Elementary, Englewood High School, George Washington High School, Ponderosa High School, Powell Middle School, Slater Elementary, Standley Lake High School, St. Jerome's Elementary, and Westridge Elementary.

TEACHERS' PREFACE

We accept the challenge of building a brighter future.
We will not ignore the problems in our society.
We pledge to work for respect for all Americans.

The Kids Explore series, written by kids for kids, is meant to be informative and to help readers learn to respect all people. The Westridge Young Writers Workshop is located at Westridge Elementary School in Jefferson County, Colorado, a suburb of Denver.

We have chosen to use young writers because students are interested in what their peers think and see. *Kids Explore the Gifts of Children with Special Needs* was written during one school year with the participation of nine different classes and their teachers. The authors are students in the third

through sixth grades. Each classroom hosted a student with special needs and worked on the chapter about that student. Everyone involved in the writing—students, teachers, and staff—grew so much personally as they came to know these children with special gifts.

While working with our featured students and families, we saw that teachers make a significant difference in how a child with special needs is accepted into the classroom. A child's success in his or her program is directly related to the teacher's ability to share information and model enthusiasm.

For example, when one of our featured students was in preschool, her teacher ignored the child's disability and the other children were afraid of the student and her leg braces. The next year, the child's kindergarten teacher stressed the uniqueness of every person, and even asked the child to pass her braces around the classroom so the other children could see what they were like. That year, the child made many friends and had a great time in school.

In every success story in our book, a creative teacher was involved in some way. Whether a teacher organizes a Circle of Friends to support a child with a disability or involves a child in a wheel-chair in playground activities, he or she makes a significant contribution to the success of each child's program.

If you enjoy reading this book, we hope you will look for our other books. *Kids Explore America's Hispanic Heritage*, *Kids Explore America's African-American Heritage*, and *Kids Explore America's Japanese-American Heritage* give insight into three of the many diverse cultures that make up our country. Watch for future titles in the Kids Explore series. We provide these resources to be used in classrooms and homes across our nation to teach respect and understanding for everyone.

THE GIFTS OF CHILDREN
WITH SPECIAL NEEDS

SHAWN LEWIS
Living with Fetal Alcohol Syndrome

Go Broncos

Fifteen-year-old Shawn Lewis is tall and thin and has a great personality. In the summer, Shawn is a special junior volunteer at Children's Hospital. He delivers flowers to people, files medical records, works in the day care center, and plays with the kids who have brothers and sisters in the hospital. He also visits patients in their rooms and helps them feel better. He does this well because he is a good listener and has a great sense of humor. Shawn knows what it's like to be in the hospital because he has been there many times himself.

Shawn has Fetal Alcohol Syndrome (FAS). This is a problem that causes birth defects in about 40,000 babies each year in our country. FAS can occur when a mom drinks alcohol during the first months of her pregnancy. The alcohol causes the healthy baby's brain and body to develop improperly. A baby with FAS might be born with learning and thinking problems, with organs that don't work right, or with weak muscles. Shawn has many of these problems.

Shawn's story began with his birth on June 17, 1977. It was apparent right away that something was wrong. His

Lori Stober

Shawn (right) with one of his friends at Medical Day Treatment School

skin was blue and his heart beat was not normal. When he was just two days old, he had the first of many open heart surgeries.

When he was 18 months old, Shawn was at home with his mom when she died of a drug overdose. He was all by himself for two days with no one to feed him, change him, or care for him. He didn't even get the heart medicine he needed. Finally, Shawn's aunt found him and took him to the hospital.

Life was hard for Shawn's dad after that. He decided he could not care for Shawn, so he took him to a foster home in Colorado. There, Shawn met his new foster family, the Lewises. The Lewis family had been asked to take Shawn home with them for a two-week trial period. During that time, the Lewises would decide if they wanted to keep Shawn or not. Shawn's foster parents fell in love with him immediately. All of the Lewis children were grown, so his new parents were sure they could give Shawn the love, time, and care that he needed. In just two days they made the decision that he would be their son forever.

When Shawn first came to live with the Lewis family, he was scared of men. Because he was only two years old, they couldn't ask him why. His new dad asked the doctor what he should do. The doctor told him not to touch or pick Shawn up. He reassured Shawn's dad that Shawn would come to him in time. One night, about a year later, the family was eating dinner. Shawn climbed down from his chair, went over to his dad, and crawled right up into his lap! His dad was so happy he cried. Today, Shawn and his dad are very close and do a lot of things together.

Even though Shawn was two years old when he came to the Lewis family, he could barely crawl and he could not walk. Most of the time he scooted from place to place. His new sister, LaDonna, was 19 years old. She would come home from work, change into her jeans, and get down on the floor to work with Shawn. She did this every day until he could walk. LaDonna was always there to support Shawn through his illnesses.

When Shawn was seven, he had two heart operations. LaDonna had planned to get married in June that year, but Shawn was still very weak from being in bed so long after the operations. The Lewis family decided to put off the wedding until July because his sister wanted Shawn to be the ring bearer. July came, and Shawn was still very tired and weak. But he was determined not to let his sister down. Shawn said he would walk by himself, and he did. He needed a little help up the stairs, but he made it down the aisle and handed them the rings. This was a good example of Shawn's determination.

Shawn's first years were filled with many operations. By the time he was 13, he had had six heart operations, two eye surgeries, and many other medical procedures. His heart was so weak that the doctors finally decided that he needed a heart transplant. Shawn's name was

Shawn (right) taking a break at school

put on a national computer list of people who need organ transplants.

On March 19, 1991, a 12-year-old boy died when a blood vessel burst in his brain. Right away, his parents donated parts of his body to help others. Shawn Lewis was to receive the boy's heart, so something that took one life gave life to another.

Shawn was at his nephew's birthday party when he got a call to go to the hospital because they had found a heart for him. Shawn's parents were very thankful, but Shawn was just plain scared. Shawn had only been on the national computer list for three days! Luck

was on Shawn's side, for the heart and tissue were a perfect match to his own. Shawn had beaten the odds again. He was taken to Children's Hospital immediately to get ready for the transplant.

As soon as Shawn and his family went to the hospital, their friends came to support them. About fifty people gathered in the waiting room of the hospital. Everyone stayed awake all night, singing and praying with the family to keep their spirits high. As Shawn's dad put it, "We did the praying while the doctors did the doctoring." They prayed for Shawn, they prayed for the boy who had lost his life, and they sent thanks to

Lori Stober

Shawn discussing school projects with classmates

the boy's parents. Shawn's parents said they will never forget the gift they were given or the courage of the boy's family.

While Shawn was in the hospital being prepared for surgery, Dr. Campbell, his heart surgeon, went to Wyoming to remove the other heart. Because of problems caused by scar tissue from previous heart surgeries, it took a long time for the doctors and nurses to open Shawn's chest and get it ready for the transplant. Dr. Campbell quickly flew back to Denver in a private plane with a cooler that contained the heart.

After they took out Shawn's heart, they hooked him up to a special machine called the Life Machine. This machine keeps the patient alive by pumping the blood through the body while the new heart is sewn in. The stitches for attaching the new heart are so small that the doctors have to use a powerful magnifying glass called a loupe to see them.

Shawn's surgery lasted eight hours, from 11:00 at night until 7:00 in the morning. When he woke up, Shawn thought that he was dead because there was no pain in his chest. For the first time, Shawn realized it wasn't normal to have pain in his chest.

After Shawn's recovery, he attended his first real school, a large middle school. What a change this was for Shawn! Before, he had had a tutor come to his home to teach him to read, write, and do math and science. They sat at the kitchen table or at the computer in Shawn's room. Science was his favorite subject, and sometimes he and his tutor did experiments in the kitchen.

At Shawn's new school, some of the hallways were nearly a block long! They were packed with hundreds of kids, and the passing time was only five minutes. Shawn sometimes had a student aide to help him walk down the long halls between classes. Shawn started with four class periods each day, but this made him too tired, so he cut back to two class periods.

The school nurse found out about a new school for kids with medical problems and told Shawn's mom about it. Mrs. Lewis investigated the Medical Day Treatment School sponsored by Children's Hospital and the Denver Public Schools. At this school, two nurses and two teachers help the kids with their studies and teach them how to care for their own health. It took Mrs. Lewis a month to get her son into this special program.

Although Shawn liked the new and smaller school at Children's Hospital, he still had some problems. Shawn was really mad when he couldn't do his multiplication and division facts. One day his

Lori Stober

Shawn and friends having lunch at school

dad found Shawn lying on his bed, very depressed. They talked about the problem, and Mr. Lewis helped Shawn realize it wasn't his fault that he couldn't learn the math facts. They came up with the idea to use a calculator to do math. Shawn talked to his math teacher about the effects of Fetal Alcohol Syndrome on his learning, and she allowed him to use the calculator. Shawn is now where he should be in math, working on geometry and algebra.

Shawn's favorite subject in school is physical education (PE). For PE, his class goes to the gym in the basement of Children's Hospital. The class starts with exercises, and then they play a sport, such as touch football, horse basketball, or even soccer. This class also takes fun field trips to do special things like ice skating and bowling. Shawn takes part for about a half-hour or as long as he

can. He only quits when he's so tired he can't go on. Wherever the class goes, a nurse is always there to help in case there are any health problems.

After just a year at the Medical Day Treatment School, Shawn was elected student body president. When kids have a problem they come talk to him. He has great ideas and he shares them during school meetings. If he sees something that needs to be changed, he helps fix it. Shawn loves it when new students come to his school because he can help them make friends.

Shawn has many friends at this school. His best friend, James, likes to watch and play football. James can't play tackle football because he has cystic fibrosis, a lung disease. James and Shawn talk on the phone a lot, but they don't get together outside of school because they live 27 miles apart.

Just like each of us, Shawn has a dream. He dreams about becoming a pilot for the Air Force. He first thought of this when he watched the movie *Top Gun*. Later, during one of his hospital stays, some Air Force Academy cadets

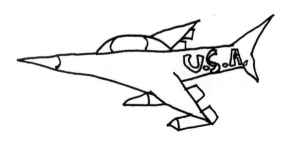

came to visit Shawn. They talked to him about his dream and encouraged him to never give up.

Shawn told us that before he had his heart transplant, he wanted to have a meeting with the doctors because he was putting his life in their hands. During the meeting, Shawn asked the doctors if he would ever be able to be a pilot. One doctor told Shawn that with a heart transplant he would probably never fly a plane. The doctor saw that this really disappointed Shawn. The doctor said, "Even though you'll have a heart transplant, don't give up your dream. Remember, we thought you

would die when you were very young, and you proved us wrong." Shawn believes he will achieve his dream. Who knows? Shawn Lewis may become the first person with a heart transplant to be an Air Force Academy cadet.

IN SHAWN'S OWN WORDS

My life has been a long, hard road, but I've got a lot to show for it. The day I had my heart transplant, well, the only thing I can compare it to is some kind of rebirth, like a phoenix rising from the ashes. It felt like a big weight had been lifted off my chest. Physically and emotionally, I just felt good all over.

This book is about people that others sometimes think are different. But we are all probably more alike than we know. I think we should accept people for who they are and not judge them by what disease or skin color they have. I can speak from experience that it's a lot nicer to hear, "Hey, wanna play ball?" than, "Oh, man, I feel so sorry for you." It's definitely a good thing to care about a friend's health and be concerned, but don't dwell on it.

When I play baseball with my friends, it feels great. It's like I'm being accepted for being me. When these kids, who are twice as healthy as I am, tell me I am an awesome ball player, it doesn't get much better than that.

QUESTIONS & ANSWERS ABOUT HEART TRANSPLANTS

We have learned a lot about heart transplants and donating organs. We want to share this information with you.

Where do doctors get the heart?
Doctors get the heart from a donor, someone who has died and arranged earlier to donate his or her organs to help others. After the doctors learn that

Lori Stober

Shawn playing whiffle ball in PE class

Lori Stober

Shawn working on a school computer with his teacher

a donor has died, they check a national computer list of people who need a healthy organ. Then they contact the patient who will be the best match for the organ.

How do the doctors determine if the donor's heart is right for a transplant patient?
The doctors check the blood type and the tissue of the heart to see if it matches the patient's blood type and tissue. They also check to see that the heart is healthy and is the right size for the patient. Size can vary greatly. A baby's

heart is about the size of a baby's fist. Shawn's heart was about as big as his two fists held together.

What do they do with the old heart?
The doctors take out the old heart and put it in a jar with preservative liquids. Then they send it to a pathologist, a doctor who specializes in the causes of disease. This special doctor studies the heart to see what was wrong with it. This research helps doctors learn how to help other people with similar heart problems.

How do the doctors decide that a person needs a heart transplant?

The doctors run a lot of tests. They might find out that a person has a bad heart by using an echo machine. This is the same machine they use to do ultrasound tests on babies in pregnant moms. To check the heart, they run the machine over the patient's chest. When the doctors determine that something is wrong with the heart that can't be fixed, they test the blood and the tissue type. Then they put the patient on the national computer list. People who are not expected to live long are put at the top of the list.

What do the doctors watch for after transplant surgery?

The biggest problem to watch for after surgery is that the body may reject the new heart. This happens when the body feels the new heart is a foreign object and does not belong. White blood cells, which work like tiny soldiers, attack the new organ and try to kill it. This is the same way the body reacts to disease. People who have had a transplant take medicine so their body will not reject the new heart. They need to do this for the rest of their lives. This medicine prevents the white blood cells from attacking the heart, but it also makes it hard for the body to fight infection and disease.

How do you become a donor?

Once you are an adult, it is easy to become a donor. When people renew their driver's license, they can simply tell the clerks that they want to become a donor. The clerk will put a little sticker on the license. Or people can call the local hospital to find out about donor organizations in the area.

If you are under 18, you have to have your parents' permission to become a donor. Shawn's parents told us that everyone needs to think about organ and tissue donation ahead of time, so that when the time comes everything has already been arranged. This way people who have lost a loved one don't have to make such a hard decision when they are very upset. People who want to become donors should discuss it with their family and friends. They should let them know what they want to donate so that their wishes will be carried out after they die.

Our Poem Dedicated to Shawn

If only people could learn to give,
Then a lot of people would be able
to live.

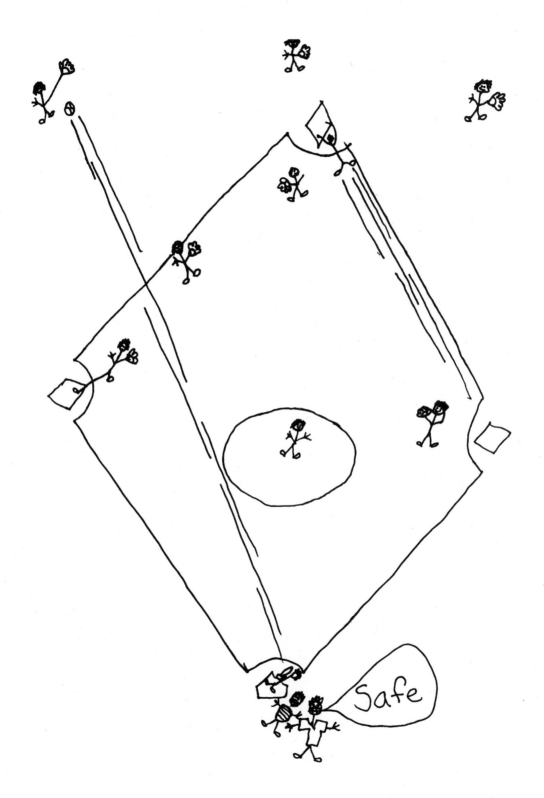

Safe

MIKELLE LEARNED
Living with Cerebral Palsy

Mikelle Learned helps others learn about disabilities. Once when she was helping present a program on disabilities, one of the students asked her if she was sad she couldn't walk. She moved her eyes to say "no," and then touched her nose and smiled. The teacher asked if she had to go to the bathroom because touching her nose was the signal for that. She said "no" again and kept the signal up until finally the teacher asked, "Do you want them to know you are happy because you can tell us you have to go to the bathroom?" Mikelle squealed and smiled.

During the compliment time at the end of the program, one kid told Mikelle that he thought the world would be a better place if we all followed her example. He said, "I'm going to try to think about what I *can* do rather than what I *can't* do." When you meet Mikelle, you see that this is how she feels about herself, too.

Mikelle has cerebral palsy (CP). Cerebral palsy is caused by damage to the brain. This is the reason that Mikelle cannot walk or talk. Don't let this fool you. Mikelle is very smart and doesn't let anything stand in her way. Mikelle's life is very interesting today, but so is her past.

Mikelle laughing at a joke

When Mikelle was just a baby, she and 12 other South Korean children traveled halfway around the world to join new families in America. Katherine and Bruce Learned, Mikelle's parents, remember the day. It was October 15, 1983, and when the 16-hour-long flight finally arrived at the gate, there was excitement in the air. The Learneds and all the other parents were about to see their adopted children for the first time. The Learneds had decided to call their child Mikelle when they saw her picture at a presentation by the Korean adoption agency. When they saw Mikelle, they knew her new name would fit her well.

The Learneds' family of three became a family of four overnight. Mikelle had a new mom, a new dad, and a new four-year-old brother named Kasey. By the end of the first day Mikelle was already a part of the family.

The Learneds soon saw that Mikelle was not growing like an average baby. Sometimes a child's growth slows down when he or she moves to a new country, but usually these children get used to their new home and begin to grow normally. But three months after her arrival, Mikelle was still very small for her age.

Mikelle's mom and dad began to see other differences between Mikelle and her brother when he was a baby. Mikelle's body was stiff, and she always kept a tight grip on anything she held. She was startled by any movement, and she liked to be held tightly. Her parents built a special box for her to make her feel secure when they laid her down. They filled the box with foam and left the top open. Mikelle felt very safe there and didn't get startled so easily.

As time went on, her parents became more worried that she was behind other kids. They made arrangements for Mikelle to get a checkup and have special tests done. That was when the doctors discovered that Mikelle had cerebral palsy. They said she needed to start physical therapy right away.

The Learneds knew the physical therapy would be hard for the whole family. The therapist came to their home with objects and equipment for Mikelle to work with. One exercise Mikelle had to do was lie on a three-foot beach ball and roll it back and forth to learn how to use her stomach muscles. Her parents and the therapist also pulled on her legs and gently bent them to strengthen them and make them more flexible. The doctors said it was important to work hard with Mikelle when she was young, so she could learn to use her muscles.

Mikelle's physical therapy was very expensive. She had to have therapy three times a week, but her family's insurance covered only a small part of it. In fact, the insurance paid for only three months of therapy, even though Mikelle would need it for most of her life. The Learneds didn't know what to do. Their daughter really needed help, but the family just couldn't afford all the medical bills.

Then something wonderful happened. Mikelle's mom heard about an organization called Easter Seals. Easter Seals helps families pay for the medical care and equipment their children need. The organization started to pay for Mikelle's therapy right away.

Sometimes Mikelle's family got discouraged because Mikelle's therapy was very difficult. But she would often surprise them with how quickly she learned. Her parents began to realize that she was a very bright child. For example, she could follow directions very well, and she was potty-trained before she was even two years old, which is earlier than many kids.

Lori Stober

Mikelle eating a snack

Mikelle got her first power wheelchair when she was just three years old. This tiny wheelchair was specially made for her. A family friend helped raise $5,000 to pay for it. Mikelle's mother was very relieved because the power chair helped Mikelle be more independent. At first, Mikelle just went in circles in the chair because she didn't have the coordination to make it go straight. Finally, she learned to make it go where she wanted. At last, she could go all over the house on her own, without being carried.

A lot of things happened to Mikelle when she was five years old. Her parents got a divorce and had to sell their house. Like many kids with divorced parents, Mikelle lives with her mother and visits her father on weekends, vacations, and holidays.

When it was time for Mikelle to go to school, her mom had trouble finding the right one for her. She first looked at a school just for disabled children, but she thought the classes were too slow for Mikelle. Even though Mikelle had many physical problems, her mind worked fine, so Mikelle's mother wanted to send her to a regular school. Finally, they found Bromwell Elementary, a school that seemed just right.

Next, Mikelle's mom found an apartment close to the new school. It

was on the seventh floor of a high-rise building near downtown Denver. This building was a good place for Mikelle because it had an elevator and a wheelchair ramp.

Mikelle's new school arranged for a bus with a wheelchair lift to pick her up. Every day, her mom had to push Mikelle across a busy street to meet the bus. This was difficult, so the school arranged for a special van called an Amb-o-cab to pick up Mikelle. The Amb-o-cab driver came right to Mikelle's apartment door every morning. After they got to the van, the driver opened the big sliding door and pulled down a ramp so that Mikelle could roll her wheelchair into the van.

During her kindergarten year, Mikelle had to have an operation on her hips to help her sit up more easily and maybe even walk. It was a very serious operation. Mikelle was in the hospital for five days and in a body cast at home for seven weeks. Mikelle still can't walk, but it is easier for her to sit up. Now

that her bones are arranged more normally, she may even be able to walk someday.

Now Mikelle is in the third grade at Bromwell Elementary. She is in a second- and third-grade combination classroom. In a combination classroom, half the kids are in one grade and half the kids are in another. Mikelle likes this because she has had the same teacher for two school years. We think she is one of the smartest kids in her class.

Mikelle does all the assignments the other kids do but in different ways. Most of the day Mikelle stays in the regular classroom. When it is time for reading, math, and writing, Ms. Keys, her teacher, assigns a partner for Mikelle. While she reads, her partner sits by her. Mikelle's book is attached to her tray with rubber bands, and she pulls on her partner's shirt or touches him or her when she needs the page turned. Mikelle does math problems using a special board on her wheelchair. First, she points to a number and then to the place value. For the number 795, for example, she points to the seven and the hundreds place, then the nine and the tens place, and then the five and the ones place.

She takes spelling tests, too. Mikelle has the same spelling words as the other kids in her class. Mikelle sees Mrs. Donaldson, a special education teacher, for about an hour a day. To test Mikelle on spelling, Mrs. Donaldson puts a sheet of words on Mikelle's wheelchair tray. Then she says a word

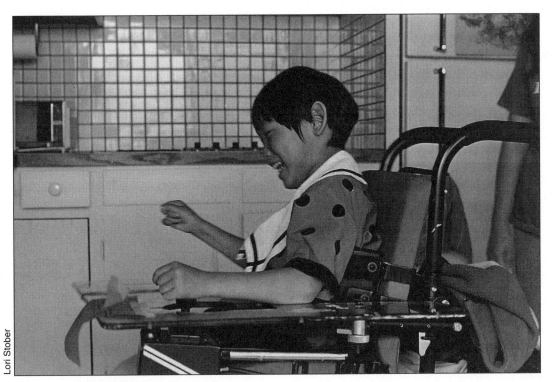

Lori Stober

Mikelle using her wheelchair at home

and Mikelle points to it on the paper. Mikelle's teacher says she gets very good grades.

Mikelle also has a machine called a touch talker to talk with the people and kids at school and other places. She doesn't use it all the time because she has other ways to communicate, and sometimes her touch talker breaks down. She pushes different buttons to make it speak a word or show it on the machine's display. The button for "knucklehead" is the one she especially likes to use when she is upset with her brother, Kasey. Mikelle's teacher helped her program that word. Mikelle can also hook her touch talker up to a printer

and print out what she wants to say.

The touch talker Mikelle uses was very expensive. Her mom wrote a letter in the school's newspaper to raise money to buy the machine. She found out later that a generous parent who has a child in Mikelle's class donated half of the money for the touch talker. The parent wouldn't tell who he or she was, but donated the money because he or she was glad that Mikelle was in the class and other children could learn from her.

Besides the touch talker, Mikelle uses signals and noises to express her feelings or to get help. When she has to go to the bathroom, she puts her finger on her nose, and someone gets the school aide to take her. If she wants a drink, she puts her finger to her mouth, and the person closest to her gets her a cup of water. When she is hungry, she rubs her stomach.

Mikelle's best friend's name is Shar, and he is in her class. Even though Mikelle can't talk, Shar and Mikelle communicate very well. Shar can almost read Mikelle's mind! Mikelle gets his attention by pulling on his shirt. Then he asks what she wants. For example, if Mikelle's wheelchair battery is dead and she needs him to push her, Mikelle looks at the back of her chair and pushes the control. Mikelle and Shar both have a great sense of humor and like to tease each other and joke around.

When Mikelle comes home from school, her brother Kasey is there. He takes care of her two days a week. Like most brothers, he doesn't enjoy babysitting, but he has to do it anyway. Sometimes his mom pays him to babysit, but he doesn't really have to do much because Mikelle takes care of most things herself. She can even get the refrigerator door open when she wants a snack. Sometimes Kasey helps her get the snack out, and she watches TV while she eats it. When she needs Kasey to take her to the bathroom, she goes and gets him, calls out, or presses the electric horn on her wheelchair.

If Mikelle gets mad at Kasey, she goes to her bedroom and locks the door. She also chases him with her wheelchair and runs over his feet.

Mikelle showed us her special signal for her brother. She made a fist with her hand and put it to her head. This signal means "knucklehead!" Mikelle and Kasey are just like other brothers and sisters. They fight, they talk, and they love each other.

Mikelle's mom told our class that she believes Mikelle will be able to live on her own one day and get a job to support herself. Mikelle and her family have a special dream. They hope she will be able to get a trained monkey to help her do more things by herself. These small monkeys, called capuchins (*KAP-you-chins*), are specially trained to help disabled people. The monkey would be able to turn the lights on and off for Mikelle, open and close doors for her, and bring her a book and turn the pages. It would even be able to put a tape into the casette player and turn it on. The monkey would be a pair of

Lori Stober

Mikelle playing with a friend

helping hands to make Mikelle more independent. When Mikelle heard her mother talk about the monkey, she broke into a huge smile and squealed. Mikelle let us know that this was a dream she wanted to come true.

IN MIKELLE'S OWN WORDS
(with help from her family)

I want everybody to know that I enjoy my life. The things that are the most important to me are my mom, my brother, my dad, my grandma, and the rest of my family and friends.

One of my favorite things to do is laugh. I love a good joke or a silly movie. I also love the color purple. I like the things I own to have some purple on them. My new wheelchair is purple, my purse is purple, and even my toothbrush is purple.

Please understand that I know that walking and talking are very hard for me, but I don't let that get in the way of my desire to do things and have friends. Please don't feel sorry for me, because I am very happy. Some people think I can't understand them, so they will talk to my mother or brother instead of to me. Mom is great about letting them know that I am smart, and that it is always better when people talk to me rather than acting like I am not there.

QUESTIONS & ANSWERS ABOUT CEREBRAL PALSY

We tried to learn as much as we could about cerebral palsy (CP). Here are some questions and answers we thought you might like to know about.

What is cerebral palsy?
Cerebral palsy is caused by damage to the brain. The major cause of CP is lack of oxygen to the baby during birth. Premature babies (babies who are born early) may also get CP if they don't get enough oxygen. If a mother has German measles during her pregnancy, her baby may get CP. Little children who get lead poisoning or a serious injury that cuts off oxygen to their brains may also develop CP.

Cerebral palsy causes many different disabilities. It usually causes a lack of muscle control and coordination. This can be anything from a mild speech problem to not being able to control any body movements at all. Many people with CP cannot walk or talk. It doesn't get worse as a person ages. CP is not contagious, and it is not hereditary. (A hereditary disease is one that is passed from a parent to a child through the genes. Genes are parts of cells that determine many traits, such as eye color and what we look like.)

What are the symptoms of CP?
The symptoms of CP are different depending on how severely the brain is damaged. Some children don't show any obvious signs of CP for a long time, but

others may have serious symptoms from birth. Some physical symptoms are poor muscle control or muscle spasms, and problems seeing and hearing. Some CP babies have a hard time sucking. CP can cause emotional problems and make babies very tense and fussy. CP makes it hard for some children to concentrate, and a few with CP may be mentally retarded.

How can we prevent CP?
It is important for women to get a shot against German measles to protect against birth defects. Pregnant women need to have regular checkups. A good diet, regular exercise, a lot of rest, avoiding alcohol and drugs, and not smoking can help mothers have healthy babies. If mothers don't do these things, their babies could be born premature and that can cause birth defects.

Is there a cure for CP?
There is no cure, but there are things that help people with CP. Medication, surgery, physical therapy, speech therapy, and counseling can help. Power chairs, special taxis and buses, cars with hand controls, touch talkers, computers, elevators, and other mechanical equipment allow people with CP to live more independent lives. Medication is used to help people who have seizures and spasms. Surgery can build better joints.

How will research help people with CP?
Researchers are working on vaccinations (shots) that can help prevent birth defects. They are looking for ways to help children with CP learn more easily. Someday researchers may find a way to help the brain send messages to muscles that aren't doing their job. These messages would make the muscles work properly.

Our Poem Dedicated to Mikelle

> *If we all had Mikelle's attitude,*
> *The world would be a brighter*
> * place.*
> *We would treat each other better,*
> *And have a smile upon our face.*

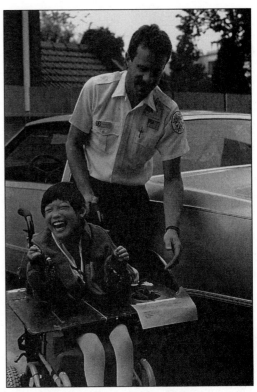

Lori Stober

The Amb-o-cab driver helping Mikelle

NATHAN MOUTRAY
Living with Dyslexia

If you came to the playground at Slater Elementary in Lakewood, Colorado, you might see Nathan Moutray solving problems. He is a student mediator and helps other kids solve arguments that come up on the playground. First, Nathan sets down rules for the students to follow. The rules include things like promising to tell the truth, not calling each other names, not interrupting, and agreeing to work hard to solve the problem. Next, Nathan asks each kid to tell his or her side of the story. He listens to both kids without taking sides. Then Nathan helps them come up with a solution they both can agree on. Once they reach a so-

lution, he asks them what they can do so that they won't have the same problem again. Nathan is a great student mediator because he is a good listener and a skilled peacemaker. If you saw Nathan at work you would never know that he has an invisible disability called dyslexia.

Dyslexia causes perception problems. Perception refers to how you understand what you see. For example, Nathan often perceives b's, p's, d's and q's as different letters because his mind thinks the stems of the letters are pointing the other way. The dyslexia affects Nathan's ability to read and write and also his coordination.

Nathan reads a taped book with his teacher, Mrs. Zo

Mark Dickson

Imagine how you would feel if all the books in your classroom suddenly had Chinese writing in them. All your classmates could read them, but you could not. You might feel frustrated, dumb, or angry. If you can imagine yourself in this situation, then you will know how our friend Nathan Moutray feels.

Before his dyslexia started affecting Nathan's reading, it affected his coordination. One day when he was just a toddler, he and his mom were walking to school to pick up his older brother from kindergarten. Nathan tripped and fell and scraped the freckles right off his nose! Today, you can still see a little shiny spot where the freckles once were.

When he was little, Nathan always put his shoes on the wrong feet. His mom asked if his feet hurt when his shoes were on wrong. Nathan said no, they looked and felt right to him. Because of these problems, Nathan's dad worried that Nathan might have learning problems like he had had. Mr. Moutray himself had struggled with reading and writing in school. Mrs. Moutray wondered why Nathan never wanted to listen to a story or practice writing or drawing. She didn't know it at the time, but Nathan's difficulty telling left from right and his short attention span were early signs that he had dyslexia.

Nathan continued to have problems when he started school. He had a hard time coloring within the lines, learning his ABC's and 1, 2, 3's, and skipping and hopping. His teacher had him practice forming his letters by writing them big in sand, and that helped a little. But Nathan still couldn't write his name on paper or put his shoes on the right feet. (His grandma put left and right identifying marks on the bottom of his shoes, but that didn't help either.)

Even though school was hard for Nathan, at home he enjoyed being a regular kid. He and his brothers built a unique treehouse in their backyard in an old cottonwood tree. It could hold four kids easily. They entered from the bottom on a ladder, and there was a pulley to lift whatever they couldn't carry up the ladder. The family's German shepherd, Macho, would climb up the ladder to the treehouse, but he couldn't climb down, so the boys would have to lower him down with the pulley. Nathan enjoyed playing in the treehouse because it took his mind off of school.

Nathan had a hard year in first grade, but he was passed to second grade. There, he had even more problems. When he tried to read, the words seemed to flip and fly. Nathan felt different because the other kids understood their lessons much more quickly than he did. But he never gave up. As Nathan

fell further behind his classmates, his parents decided he should repeat second grade. Repeating a grade made Nathan feel sad inside.

Later that summer, Nathan's family moved to a house near Slater Elementary. Nathan felt bad because he was leaving his friends and his treehouse behind. But one good thing about the move was that no one at the new school knew he was repeating second grade. When Nathan couldn't remember what he had learned the first time in second grade, he realized something was wrong. He began to wonder if he was dumb. He wondered why he couldn't read and why he forgot over the summer what he had learned during the school year. Nathan felt better when he made a new best friend, named Jack Wright. Nathan and his older brother Shawn also found a lake near their new house where they could play and fish.

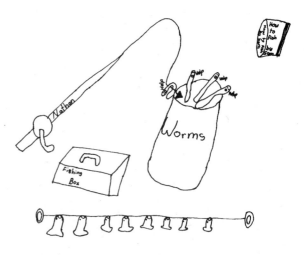

Nathan shows his teacher a story he is writing on the computer

School got harder for Nathan. Reading and writing frustrated him more and more, and he got nervous even trying to do them. Sometimes Nathan felt angry because school was so difficult. It seemed like no matter how hard he tried, he just couldn't keep up with his class. Because Nathan had so much trouble, he started going to a special class.

This is when Nathan met Mrs. Zo. She is a creative person who teaches kids with learning disabilities. She encourages Nathan. When he gets depressed, she reminds him how smart he really is. Mrs. Zo told him, "Nathan you just learn differently, and we will find the way that you learn the best. Just think about how well you do in math."

In addition to reassuring him, Mrs. Zo helps Nathan by presenting information to him in different ways. Because Nathan has trouble reading, she encourages him to use his ears more than his eyes to learn. Once he hears something, he understands it. Mrs. Zo helps Nathan by using taped books, which are books read aloud on tape. Nathan picks a book he likes and, as he listens to it, he follows the printed words in the book. If Nathan perceives a written word different from the way it is read aloud, he

knows he has read it incorrectly and can learn the right word. In this way, Nathan is able to read more challenging books. Mrs. Zo has hundreds of books on tape for Nathan to choose from. If he wants to read a book that is not on tape, Mrs. Zo gets a volunteer to record it for him.

Mrs. Zo also helps Nathan with his writing on the computer. When Nathan uses the computer, the key he types is the letter that gets printed, so he doesn't have to worry about how to form the letter by hand. Another way she helps Nathan to write is by having him say his stories out loud into a tape recorder. After Nathan records his story, he slowly plays it back and writes it down. Because the tape recorder saves his thoughts for him, Nathan can concentrate on writing the letters and words correctly. The tape recorder and the computer have helped Nathan to improve in both reading and writing.

Spelling is also really tough for Nathan. Often he has to stop and look at the chart on the classroom wall that shows how to write the letters of the alphabet, but then he may forget what comes next. For example, if he is writing the word "day," he forgets how to make the letter "d." When he looks at the chart to see a "d," he forgets the word he is trying to write. Because spelling is so hard, Nathan likes to do his work on the computer as much as he can because the spell checker is a big help.

Nathan keeps trying hard in school because he knows a teacher who has dyslexia and who can now read well. This gives him hope that one day he will be able to read well, too.

Although Nathan has trouble in school, he prides himself on being very mechanical. He helps his dad, who is a tree trimmer. They use a truck called a highranger that has a bucket on the end of a long pole. The bucket is big enough

Mark Dickson

Nathan helps his dad

Mark Dickson

Nathan works with a fourth grade author on his story for the book

to hold a person up high in the air to trim trees. The controls that raise and lower the bucket are hard to use, but Nathan can operate them.

There's an old saying that reminds us of Nathan: "Winners never quit, and quitters never win." Nathan will never quit trying to learn to read and write. Nathan knows it is tough, but he never gives up. We know Nathan is a winner.

IN NATHAN'S OWN WORDS

I hope that people learn not to make fun of others with dyslexia and other learning problems. I want people to treat everyone who has disabilities with respect. Remember that people with dyslexia are not stupid, they have an invisible disability. I want everyone to know that dyslexics are not lazy, they try really hard. They may learn differently, but they can learn!

QUESTIONS & ANSWERS ABOUT DYSLEXIA

We learned many things about dyslexia that we want to share with you.

What is dyslexia?
"Dyslexia" is a medical word. We think

Mark Dickson

Nathan explains to the fourth grade authors how reading is difficult for him

"dyslexic" is a strange word to describe people who have trouble reading because it is hard to read. People with dyslexia have trouble reading, writing, or talking, because their brains have a defect that makes them perceive things incorrectly.

Some scientists believe that dyslexia is caused by how the two sides of the brain grow. In most people, both sides of the brain grow at about the same speed. In dyslexics, the left half of the brain may develop more slowly. This is the part of the brain that handles language.

Are all dyslexics alike?

No two people are the same, and no two dyslexics are exactly alike. Dyslexia affects different people in different ways. Some dyslexics have a hard time reading and writing, but they speak very well. Others have trouble speaking and cannot seem to find the right word to put in a sentence. Some dyslexics are good at math while others have trouble reading numbers.

Who gets dyslexia?

Anyone can get dyslexia. It is estimated that one out of every ten Americans has this learning problem. More boys get

Mark Dickson

Nathan and his brother Kevin show off one of the chickens they raise

dyslexia than girls. Dr. Baron, a doctor who studies dyslexia, says this is because girls' brains develop sooner than boys'.

People of different races and people from all over the world get dyslexia. A Japanese child with dyslexia has the same problems reading, writing, and speaking Japanese as an American child with dyslexia has with English.

How do you get dyslexia?
The most common way to get dyslexia is to inherit it through genes passed down to you from your parents and grandparents. We inherit lots of things, such as our looks, our size, our blood type, and certain diseases. (Nathan may have inherited dyslexia from his dad.)

You can also get dyslexia from brain damage. Brain damage can be caused by a disease, a tumor in the head, a head injury, or a lack of oxygen. You might get a head injury in a car accident, for example, or by falling out of a high tree, or wiping out on your skateboard without your helmet on.

How serious is dyslexia?
Dyslexia cannot make you sick, but it can be very frustrating because it makes learning difficult. For example, when Nathan gets upset at his homework, he gets moody and sometimes kicks his

bed. He used to cry and scream because he was so frustrated, but now that he understands his problem, life is easier for him.

What is the difference between a slow learner and a dyslexic?

Dyslexics usually have average or above-average intelligence. A slow learner has limited ability because they have below-average intelligence. Dyslexics have the ability to do difficult tasks. However, sometimes the normal ways of receiving information, such as through reading, don't work for them.

What is it like to have dyslexia?

Having dyslexia can be like having a bad dream, especially when you don't know what is wrong. If you want to see what it's like for some dyslexics, try these two experiments.

First, try to read the sentence below.

Het stocma ta uor slocoh, Realst Meanalraty, is na gilartoal.

Now turn the page upside down to see what it really says.

ꞁoʇɐƃᴉllɐ uɐ sᴉ 'ʎɹɐʇuǝɯǝꞁƎ
ɹǝʇɐꞁS 'ꞁooɥɔs ɹno ʇɐ ʇoɔsɐɯ ǝɥ┴

For the second experiment, you will need a book and a small mirror. Hold the mirror on top of the page so the print is reflected in the mirror. Then try to read the print in the mirror. The letters in the reflection flip-flop, and they even move if you don't hold the mirror still.

This is similar to what some dyslexics see whey they look at words. For you, this might be kind of fun, but imagine how you would feel if letters always looked like this to you. What if every time you read it was like trying to figure out a secret code? We think it would be pretty tough.

We know there is a lot more to learn about dsylexia. We hope you will take the time to read some books about kids with dyslexia and do some research on it. This information is just a beginning.

Our Poem Dedicated to Nathan

> *No matter how hard the words*
> *may be to read,*
> *We don't all learn at quite the*
> *same speed.*
> *Getting an education is not a*
> *race,*
> *Hang in there and set your own*
> *pace.*

Nathan fishing with his brothers, Shawn (left) and Kevin, at a lake near his home

LISA FERRERIO
Living with Brittle Bone Disease

As soon as Lisa woke up, she knew it would be a special day. Hurrying out of bed, she wondered what she should wear. She kept saying to herself over and over, "I'm going to see Michael Jackson tonight!"

Lisa's mom and her Aunt Alice took her to the concert. As they entered Mile High Stadium in Denver, Colorado, they saw an enormous crowd. Lisa looked at her watch. The concert wouldn't start for another 25 minutes. She could hardly wait for the performance to begin! Lisa is usually in a wheelchair because she has a brittle bone disease called osteoge-

nesis imperfecta (OI). But on this special day, Aunt Alice volunteered to carry Lisa so she could see over the crowd.

When her aunt suddenly caught a glimpse of Michael Jackson, she jerked. Lisa felt her arm snap and knew what had happened. Her arm had broken! There wasn't time to go to the hospital and still see the concert, so Lisa insisted on staying. Her mom and aunt used a belt to make a sling for her arm. Even with Lisa's arm broken they stayed and watched all three hours of the concert. When it was over, Lisa and her family went to the hospital. On the way there, Lisa said, "I had a really great time."

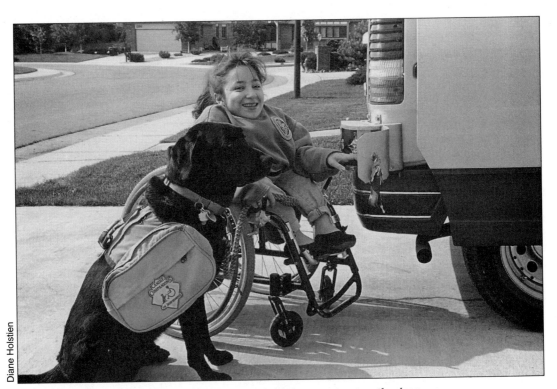

Diane Holstien

Lisa, with Kosmo, using the special box on her van's bumper to open the door

Lisa Ferrerio, a talkative 17-year-old, has a disability, but she does not let it stop her from reaching her goals. She has a 3.88 grade point average and participates in many school activities. In fact, Lisa is such a great student that she was invited to appear on a local TV program as "Student of the Week." When our class saw her on television, she caught our attention because she is so proud and so little. She is only three feet tall.

Whenever you see Lisa, you also see Kosmo, her companion dog. He was right there by her side on the television program, pulling her around the school and helping her at home. Lisa shared her cheery, positive attitude with us. She told us that she enjoys her life and doesn't feel sorry for herself.

Lisa was born on September 17, 1975. She wouldn't stop crying, and after an hour of bloodcurdling screams, the doctors knew something was wrong. They ran tests and took X-rays, and finally learned that Lisa had OI. OI is a very rare disease that makes bones very weak—so weak that just being born can break several of them. During her birth, Lisa broke both of her legs and fractured her skull.

The doctors told Lisa's parents about her disease. They said it is usually

inherited from a person's family, but they couldn't find anyone in Lisa's family who had the disease. Lisa's parents were told that the disease would also probably slow down Lisa's growth and turn the whites of her eyes bluish. But the Ferrerios also found out that Lisa was lucky. Some babies born with a very severe case of the disease die at birth. Lisa went home from the hospital in a body cast that covered her chest and both legs.

Lisa's family carried her around on a pillow because they were afraid of breaking more of her bones. In time, she sat up like a regular baby and began to crawl. She started walking when she was about two years old, but she soon learned that she needed help to walk. She often fell down and broke a bone. When she was three, she got crutches to help her walk, but she still fell a lot. By the time she was three, Lisa had broken more than fifty bones. These years were hard for everyone in her family. Lisa's breaks were extremely painful,

and she had to go right to the hospital to have casts put on them.

Even with brittle bone disease Lisa did many things other children do. She really liked dolls when she was little and played house and dress-up with them. She collected Strawberry Shortcake Dolls, and she still has at least twenty of them. Lisa liked to go to her grandparents' house. Her grandma gave her workbooks to play with, and Lisa pasted little stars and stickers on them. She liked to ride her tricycle, too, but one time when she fell off, she broke both of her legs and one arm.

Even using crutches, Lisa often tripped when she walked. Because she fell so often, her parents decided she should use a wheelchair. In first grade, Lisa started using one. That year, she also had operations to have rods put in her arms and legs to strengthen them. She has not broken so many bones since she had the operations and started using a wheelchair.

Lisa's parents were divorced when she was eight, but they are still friends and both are very supportive of their daughter. Lisa often goes out to dinner and to movies with her dad. She says he is a good cook and she loves his turkey and gravy dinners. Lisa's father, Tom Ferrerio, works for an airline, so he and Lisa can fly for free. They have gone to many different places, including Florida, Hawaii, and California. One time on the plane, a flight attendant kept coming by and asking Lisa's dad to put his black carry-on luggage in the overhead com-

Diane Holstein

Lisa doing homework with a little help from her stepdad

partment. The third time she asked, Kosmo raised his head and scared her. The flight attendant had not realized the black thing lying by Lisa's feet was not a carry-on bag but Lisa's companion dog!

When Lisa was ten, her mom married Alan Holstein, an engineer. Lisa remembers the wedding. She was the maid-of-honor and wore a pink and cream-colored dress. Lisa was an only child until her mom remarried. She now has a stepbrother named Justin who spends every other weekend at her house. Mr. Holstein and Lisa are good friends. He is very intelligent, and spends lots of time helping Lisa with her math, chemistry, and other science

courses. He has helped in other ways, too. He built ramps into the house for Lisa's wheelchair. Each week, Lisa and her stepdad watch the television show *Home Improvement* together.

Lisa and her mom, Diane Holstein, have a very close relationship. They love to shop together. Mrs. Holstien shortens Lisa's pants and shirts. Lisa even planned a surprise fortieth birthday party for her mom. Mrs. Holstein works at a photography studio in a large mall. Before Lisa could drive, her mom would pick her up after school and bring her to the studio at the mall until she was done with work.

Diane Holstein

Lisa with Kosmo and Shaffer (left), the other family dog

Lisa remembers the day when, quite by accident, she found out about companion dogs. She was 13 years old at the time. Her mom was pushing her wheelchair in the mall, when they saw a woman with a companion dog. They started talking, and the woman told Lisa and her mom how to apply for a companion dog so Lisa could be more independent.

Lisa and her mom thought this was a great idea. They contacted the Canine Companions for Independence (CCI). The agency asked Lisa for doctors' reports, letters of recommendation, and other information.

Lisa worked hard to get all of this information to CCI. When the agency called her and said she was on a waiting list for a dog, she was thrilled. But she waited and waited, and nothing happened. After three months her mom called again. CCI said it would still take more time. Lisa waited for 2½ years! She was getting very discouraged, but she was determined to get a dog.

The call from CCI finally came. They told Lisa there was an opening for her in the February training class. She could hardly wait. She was both excited and scared. She hoped her new dog would get along with her two cats, and she worried that the dog might jump on her and break her bones.

Before she knew it, Lisa was in San Diego in a room with three trainers, seven disabled people, and 12 dogs. For the first three days, each person trained with a dog for 20 minutes and then worked with a different dog. This way the trainers could tell if the dogs matched the individuals. By the third day Lisa was anxious to be given her own dog. She secretly hoped it would be the shiny black labrador named Kosmo. When they assigned him to her she was so happy, and she tried very hard to work well with Kosmo. She knew that if they didn't do well together, the trainers would give her a different dog.

Kosmo and Lisa practiced many commands, such as turning the lights on and off, picking things up, and getting around in public places. Kosmo wore a special backpack that Lisa held on to. As Kosmo walked in front of Lisa, he pulled her along behind him. They went to malls, a basketball game, and restaurants. They even went to see a movie (Kosmo snored through the whole thing!). All of a sudden, the 14 days of training were over, and Lisa and Kosmo were headed back home.

Lisa was very glad to be home to show off her new dog. But she couldn't let anyone touch him at first. In fact, no one but Lisa could pet, have eye contact with, or feed Kosmo for two weeks.

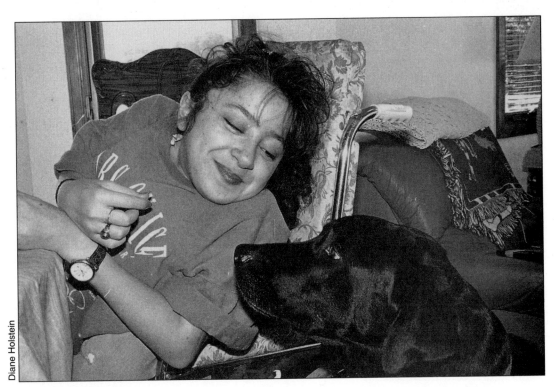

Diane Holstein

Lisa playing with Kosmo

This was so Kosmo would bond with Lisa and only Lisa.

Lisa now has a constant companion to help her be much more independent. Kosmo is trained to protect Lisa, and so she is no longer afraid to stay home alone. He sleeps in her room and goes everywhere with her. Lisa feels that, for her, having a loving companion dog is more important than being able to walk.

Lisa and Kosmo were chosen to be on a television program called *Reading Rainbow*. This is a children's television show about books. Lisa and Kosmo were used as a good example of how much a dog can do to help a disabled person. The program showed Kosmo picking things up, getting a can of pop out of the fridge, turning the lights on and off, and bringing in the groceries from the car. It also showed how Kosmo helps Lisa when they are shopping. He gives the store clerk the money for what Lisa is buying. Lisa explained to the kids that you should

never pet or feed a companion dog without asking its owner first.

Kosmo is not Lisa's only best friend. Before Kosmo came into Lisa's life, she had many other friends. She met her best friend in junior high school. Just a few days into seventh grade, Yoxa *(YOH-sah)* came into the English class and noticed that a new person, Lisa, was sitting where she had sat the day before. Later on during the class, the English teacher asked Yoxa to show Lisa around the school. Yoxa agreed and started pushing Lisa through the hallways. The girls hit it off, and in only a few weeks Lisa asked Yoxa to be her best friend. Yoxa said, "Great!"

Just like Yoxa, when Lisa turned 15 she was excited about learning to drive. In a regular car, Lisa's legs don't reach the pedals, so her parents found a special van for her that is already set up for a person with special needs. It is equipped with a hand control for the brakes and the gas, and has a box on the back bumper where Lisa puts her key in to open the door. When the door opens, Lisa pulls a lever and a ramp comes down. Next, she rolls on to the ramp and pushes a button to raise the ramp to the van door. She then rolls off the ramp and closes the door. Finally, she wheels over to the driver's seat and slides herself onto it. When Lisa drives, she keeps one hand on the steering wheel and the other on a special handle for the brakes and gas. This handle looks a little like the hand brake on a bike. Lisa also has a car phone in case of emergency. She

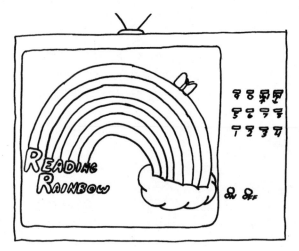

Diane Holstein

Lisa lowers the ramp on her van

uses this phone to let her mom know she has gotten to school safely.

Lisa and Yoxa are still best friends. During their junior year in high school, Stacey, a funny, bright girl from Chicago, moved to the Denver area. Stacey was in many of the same classes as Lisa and Yoxa, and all three of them soon became the best of friends.

On weekends, the girls do lots of things together. They play Bingo, go to the movies, eat out, or shop at the mall. Sometimes they just stay at home to play cards, watch television, or play board games. The girls spend as much time together as they can, and both Stacey and Yoxa love having Kosmo around.

On most school days at Standley Lake High School, you will find Kosmo pulling Lisa down the hall, with Stacey and Yoxa close by. The girls, now seniors, might be talking about preparing for a math test or what they are doing in chemistry. Usually they eat lunch together in an empty classroom so other students do not trip over Kosmo. When they are finished eating, Stacey takes Kosmo out to go to the bathroom. Stacey thinks it is neat because Kosmo is the only dog she knows that pees on command!

Because of Lisa's love for science, she wants to be an environmental engineer. She is doing an internship at Rocky Flats, a nearby industrial plant, to

find out what this job would be like. She works two hours a day, four days a week. She designs charts and graphs on a computer. After high school, Lisa is planning to go to the Colorado School of Mines. So far she has received three scholarships to attend this school.

Yoxa is also planning to be an engineer. Since Yoxa, Lisa, and Kosmo are such good friends, they're going to be roommates. The two girls went to an orientation at the Colorado School of Mines and can't wait to start college.

If others think that Lisa's disability makes her sad or discouraged, they are wrong. If you ever meet Lisa, she won't be frowning, she'll be smiling, because she has a good head on her shoulders, a good dog, and a good life.

IN LISA'S OWN WORDS

Having a physical disability does not mean that a person cannot be successful in whatever he or she pursues. Being successful in school or in a career doesn't depend on your physical state, it depends on your mental state.

There are some benefits to being disabled that some people don't consider. One benefit for me is having Kosmo always by my side. The love and support from my family and friends has also been a great benefit. I have also developed a very positive outlook on life. Having a positive attitude has helped me overcome my disability. In fact, I believe a positive attitude can help overcome anything.

QUESTIONS & ANSWERS ABOUT COMPANION DOGS

In the other chapters we have featured questions and answers about a disability. But brittle bone disease is so rare there is not a lot of information about it, except in medical books with very big words. Lisa's doctor even needed to re-

Diane Holstein

Lisa and friends studying at school

search the disease before he talked with her about it because he had never had a patient with it before. So we decided to share information with you about companion dogs, instead.

What is Canine Companions for Independence (CCI)?
CCI is a national group that provides companion dogs to help people with special needs. There are six CCI Centers across the nation. If you want to help or find out more information, write or call the CCI National Office, 4350 Occidental Road, P.O. Box 446, Santa Rosa, California 95402-0446, (707) 528-0830 V/TDD. (The letters V/TDD refer to a special phone for people who are hearing impaired.)

How does a dog become a CCI companion?
These dogs are specially bred and raised to be companion dogs. They are usually golden retrievers, German shepherds, and Labrador retrievers. This is because these breeds are kind, patient, and easy to train. Sometimes breeders donate their puppies to the organization. Then they are carefully raised by skilled, loving trainers. In two years, the dogs learn to obey a total of 89 commands. The dog then graduates from the academy, like you will graduate from high school.

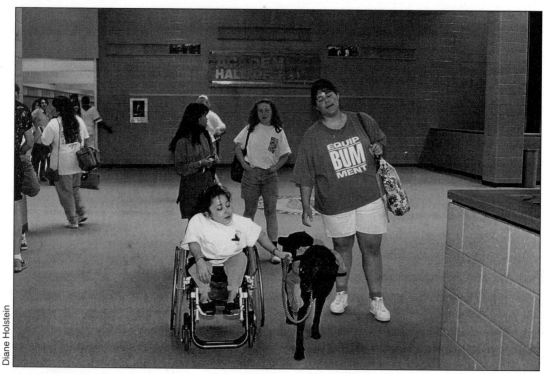

Lisa and Kosmo going down the hall at Standley Lake High School

Diane Holstein

CCI raises funds to train companion dogs. It costs about $10,000 to train each dog.

How can you get a CCI dog?
To get a CCI dog you need to contact the center nearest you to find out about the requirements. Each center has its own requirements. Only someone who has a disability can get a companion dog. People must prove that they have a need for a dog and can care for it. There is a $25 application fee and a $100 "boot camp" training fee, but the dog is given to the person free of charge.

Our Poem Dedicated to Lisa

Lisa and Kosmo make a wonder-
ful team,
Together they share a meaningful
dream.
Because they work so hard every
day,
We know they will find success on
their way.

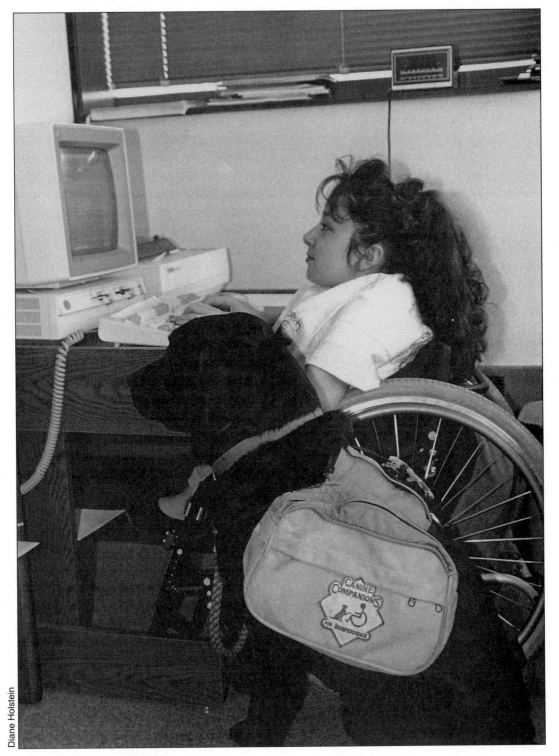

Lisa working at her computer

LANCE PETRILLO
Living with Attention Deficit Hyperactivity Disorder

Often you can't tell just by looking at someone that they have a disability or a special need. We think it would be very hard to have a problem that doesn't show because it would be hard to explain. It would also be hard to ask for help with something others can't see. Our friend Lance Petrillo has had to learn to handle an invisible disability. Lance has Attention Deficit Hyperactivity Disorder (ADHD). This makes it very hard for him to concentrate on what he is doing and to pay attention to what he is learning. Others can learn from the problems Lance has had to face in his life.

Lance remembers that when he was younger he sometimes wanted to die and go to heaven. He once said, "Life on earth stinks!" Today Lance has overcome all these feelings and is very happy. If you were to see Lance in his classroom, he would be doing many wonderful things. He might be helping his high math group work on a special project or presenting a book report to the class. He might be writing thank you notes for the group because he is one of the best writers in the class. He might be tutoring friends or helping other students settle a disagreement. You would see a determined student whose heart is very big.

Mark Dickson

Lance enjoys bowling in a league

Lance was five when he started kindergarten—and he hated it! He cried when he had to go to school. He couldn't sit still and pay attention, and even the smallest things would upset him and make him cry. He didn't have any friends, and it seemed like he was always in trouble.

Lance's teacher and parents decided that he should repeat kindergarten. He went to a brand new school and had a new teacher. This teacher was concerned about Lance because he acted younger than his age and did not do his work. Lance had mild cerebral palsy (CP), but his teacher and parents knew that it was not the cause of his behavior problems. Mr. and Mrs. Petrillo took him to doctor after doctor, trying to find out what was wrong. That year was a little better because the teacher gave him extra help.

Lance had a hard time during first and second grade. He had trouble sitting still and would talk in class when it wasn't his turn. His teachers tried to help him, but not much changed. He always wanted attention and couldn't get his work done.

Even though Lance really liked his teacher in third grade, school was hard for him. Sometimes he went to school

feeling happy, but his mood changed quickly. He didn't think that his classmates liked him, so he tried to act cool. Lance always wanted lots of attention. In third grade things started out well for Lance, but then suddenly fell apart. Lance felt like nobody was listening to him, and he couldn't take it anymore. He ran home from school and cried all the way. When he got home, he told his Mom how he felt. He thought everything would always be bad, and he didn't want to live. Lance and his mom were so upset that they cried together. Lance was so sad that even when he cheered up a little he still felt bad inside. No one seemed to know how to help him. Mr. and Mrs. Petrillo decided they had to get Lance some help from somebody.

In fourth grade, his classmates noticed something new. Lance wasn't talking loudly or out of turn, and his grades were rapidly improving. They were all surprised and proud of him. They asked Lance what had changed. He told them that his new doctor had found out that he had ADHD. The doctor helped his family learn to work with Lance and gave him some medicine that helps people with ADHD calm down and concentrate. It made a big change in Lance. At last, he was able to sit still and pay attention to his work.

With the help of the medicine, and support from his family and teachers, Lance gained more control of himself. His classmates began to hang out with him because he was calm and friendly, not wild and crazy like he had been before. Friends started to invite him over to their houses to play or to spend the night.

Because he is hyperactive, Lance has lots of energy and can play for a long time. His parents keep him active in sports as a way to use up some of his energy. He has been involved in bowling, basketball, baseball, soccer, and swimming. Lance started bowling when he was five and has done very well in this sport. He even bowls in tournaments. Recently he won eighth place in a city-wide bowling tournament.

Once, Lance joined a baseball team. Some people thought he looked silly when he ran. His hat flew off all the time and his CP made his leg movements jerky. The umpire thought Lance was just goofing around and got mad at him. When Lance's coach told the um-

Mark Dickson

Lance shares his baseball card collection with his classmates

pire about the CP, the umpire understood how hard Lance had to work to run to first base. He and the other umpires decided to give Lance an Achievement Award for trying so hard. This award had been given only three other times in the league. It was a great honor and helped Lance gain more confidence in himself.

Lance has found yet another way to be involved in sports. He collects sports cards. He has at least 6,000 cards in his collection, and it is getting bigger all the time. Lance has two cards that are very valuable. His favorite card is a second-year Michael Jordan. Lance told us that this card is worth about $175 and increases in value every month. He also has an Emitt Smith card worth $70. Lance takes good care of his cards. He wants to keep collecting until the day he dies. In fact, someday we hope to go to Lance's Collector's Shop to buy some sports cards.

IN LANCE'S OWN WORDS

When I didn't know that I had a disability, it was hard to get along with people. I knew something was wrong, but I didn't know what. I felt like people thought that I was just trying to be bad.

I was very lucky because my parents seemed like they went halfway around the world to find out what was wrong with me. They never gave up. Since they did this for me, we found out that my problem is ADHD. Since I got help, I know how to listen, pay attention, and sit still. It's important that you find help when you have a problem. With a little help and encouragement from my friends, I now continue in sports and get good grades in school.

QUESTIONS & ANSWERS ABOUT ATTENTION DEFICIT DISORDER

We had a special doctor come to school to talk to us about Attention Deficit Hyperactivity Disorder (ADHD), Lance's disability, and Attention Deficit Disorder (ADD). He explained the difference between these two conditions and then referred to both as ADD. We have done the same.

What are ADD and ADHD?
People with ADD and ADHD have trouble paying attention and concentrating. Their brains act differently and cause them to forget a lot of things. When a kid with ADD hears something, the information fades away quickly and is forgotten, like a snowflake that lands on your hand and melts in seconds.

In people with ADD, the command center of the brain does not work right. This center should tell the other parts of the brain what to pay attention to and what to ignore. But the brain of a person with ADD fails to tell the other parts of the brain what to ignore, so the person does not know what is and is not important. For example, a kid with ADD might think that listening to someone tapping a pencil is just as important as paying attention to what the teacher is saying.

What's the difference between ADD and ADHD?

Kids with ADD and ADHD all have an Attention Deficit Disorder. People who have ADHD have Attention Deficit Disorder *and* are hyperactive. They find it very difficult to sit still, and they wiggle and squirm a lot. Hyperactive people don't need as much sleep as others, and they are always on the go. A person with ADD has only Attention Deficit Disorder and is not hyperactive.

What causes ADD?

ADD is usually inherited, meaning it is passed from one generation to the next through the genes. For example, if one of your parents or one of their relatives has this problem, you could inherit it from them. When a condition can be inherited, it is said to be "hereditary."

People can also get ADD from a brain injury or from lead poisoning. Some people who have epilepsy take medication that can cause them to act like they have ADD. Some doctors believe that pregnant women who use drugs or alcohol risk having babies with ADD.

Mark Dickson

Lance and his classmates pick out books to read to their second grade buddies

Do you have ADD your whole life?
Some kids who have ADD grow out of it when they get older. Other people with ADD have it their whole life.

Why do kids with ADD always seem to be getting into trouble?
Kids with ADD can get into trouble more easily than other kids because they are forgetful and often act without thinking. For example, if a classmate tells them to hide somebody's jacket, they will probably do it without stopping to think about it. But if someone talks to them about whether or not this is a good idea, they will probably think about it and know it is wrong. Also, children with ADHD have so much energy, they fidget a lot and don't pay at-

tention to instructions. This can get them into trouble, too.

How do people with ADD act?
Remember that all people with ADD do not act the same way, because they all have different personalities and habits. Their behavior also depends on how serious their disability is.

Some kids with ADD talk out of turn because they have a hard time controlling their impulses. But not all ADD kids talk out. Others just don't pay attention and quietly do something other than what they're supposed to do. Remember that it is important not to label kids.

One thing that surprised us is that nothing seems to be true all the time. Sometimes people with ADD *can* concentrate if they are really, really interested in what they're doing. But most of the time they have trouble paying attention to one thing for more than a few minutes.

There is much to learn about this problem. We hope that you will continue to read and find out more. Many doctors are doing research to find out the cause and how to cure ADD and ADHD. We are hoping that a cure will come soon.

Our Poem Dedicated to Lance

> *Lance is really rough and tough,*
> *He's been through a lot of stuff.*
> *His family kept searching for*
>   *better ways,*
> *So that Lance would have*
>   *brighter days.*

Mark Dickson

Lance and his friend Cody talk at school

DAVID BILLARS
Living with Down Syndrome

The Billars family could be the family who lives next door to you. Mr. Billars is an electrical engineer. Mrs. Billars is a nurse who takes care of old people in their homes. They have four children. Sarah and Mike are doctors. Lianne is studying to be a nurse.

The youngest son, David, is a 13-year-old seventh grader who wants to work for Martin Marietta, a huge engineering company, when he grows up. His hair is sandy brown, his eyes are blue, and he wears glasses. He is quite tall and thin. Like other teenagers, he has chores at home. He has to clean his room, do the dishes, and help his dad mow the lawn and work on the cars. He likes to go to the mall and play video games, and he loves sports. He likes to ride his bike, go to the mountains, and take trips. David has a good sense of humor and loves to laugh. David also has Down syndrome. Down syndrome is a birth defect that causes a person to grow and learn more slowly than others. One out of every 700 babies born in our country has this disability.

David looks and sounds a little different from other kids his age. His eyes are a little slanted, and his speech is sometimes hard to understand. After

Mark Dickson

David loves to play his drums

reading this chapter, we hope you realize that although David may look different, inside he has the same feelings we do.

David was born on June 9, 1979, at 5:01 in the afternoon. He weighed 5 pounds and 12 ounces and was 18 inches long. The doctors told David's parents they thought something might be wrong because he had some features that looked like Down syndrome. The doctors did genetic testing and found that he did have this disability. Some babies born with Down syndrome have heart or stomach problems. David was quite healthy, but the doctors said he needed to start physical therapy as soon as possible to help his muscle development.

David was a very happy baby. He didn't make many noises in his crib, so his family played with him and talked to him a lot to help him learn to talk. He started therapy when he was only seven weeks old. The speech therapist helped David to strengthen the muscles in his mouth. This helped David swallow more easily and make sounds more clearly. David also had to have physical therapy to strengthen the muscles in his arms and legs, and to build up the small muscles in his hands and fingers. This gave him the ability to build with

David plays with his dog, Molly

and dad wanted him to go to a regular school, so he started second grade at a school about a mile from his home. Even in the new school, he spent most of his day in a special education class. Sixth grade was David's best year. His special education teacher taught with his regular teacher in the same classroom, and he had friends to play with. He didn't have to leave the classroom for any special classes, and he got to know his classmates better. David's favorite part of sixth grade was when they studied Greek mythology. At the end of the unit they ate Greek food, sang songs, and danced Greek dances. David liked being in a classroom with regular kids.

David met his best friend, Ryan, at this school. Like all best friends, he and Ryan spend as much time together as they can. They like to play Nintendo, play the drums, sleep over, and go trick-

blocks, color pictures, and, in time, print the letters of the alphabet. David's family helped him practice what the therapists were teaching him.

When David was a toddler, he liked to swing, ride in the seat on the back of his mom's bike, and go for wagon rides. He loved to make pretend phone calls and play in sand piles.

David got a puppy when he was three and named her Molly. David would sit on the floor, and Molly would run around him. David liked Molly so much, he had to check out her doghouse. One day he crawled into Molly's doghouse to look around. What a surprise it was for David's mother to find him stuck in Molly's house!

From the time David was three until he was eight, he went to a school for kids with special needs. But his mom

Mark Dickson

Having a picnic with friends from school

or-treating together. They like movies and doing Special Olympics. In one school program, they dressed up like bears and together lip-synced the song "Bare Necessities" from the movie *The Jungle Book*. Since they are such good friends, David can understand Ryan even though Ryan has a speech problem.

David and Ryan go to the same church. Once, they took part in a musical play called *Magic Moments*. This was a fund-raiser for the special religious education program sponsored by Father Freeman, a Catholic priest. In the play, the kids sang and wore costumes. One year, David had his picture on the front page of a Catholic newspaper

telling about this program. Father Freeman plans lots of neat things for the kids he works with. In fact, David and Ryan went on a trip to Disneyland with the group.

When David started middle school, it was scary for him. Mrs. Billars asked a neighbor kid to walk David to school to make sure he got there safely. David was afraid to go into such a big building with so many kids. He had never used a locker before and had to switch classes several times. He didn't know his way around, and he often got lost.

Miss Wachter, a special education teacher, saw the problems that David and other students with disabilities

Mark Dickson

David and his Circle of Friends

were having. She decided to ask other kids to help by joining a special group called Circle of Friends. This group supports a student with a disability. David became a member of one of these groups. There are 24 seventh-graders in David's circle who share his time and company. Each morning, some of his friends from the group wait for David at the top of a hill and walk with him across a footbridge on the way to school. When David is alone, he sometimes walks under the bridge because he doesn't like heights. But when his friends meet him, they start talking with him and he forgets he is even going across the bridge. When they get to school, other buddies meet him at his locker.

If you looked for David and his friends on a Wednesday morning around 10:00, you would find them all in a small room next to the library at Powell Middle School. First, Miss Wachter takes roll call, then they do "celebrations." This is when they talk about the things David did well during the past week. David calls on people as they raise their hands. Each person gives David a compliment, and he thanks them. It's great to celebrate a simple thing like saying "hi" to people in the hall. After celebrations, the group talks about what David needs to work on. David's friends are there to support and help him. They talk to each other about some of his problems and figure out the solutions together. At the end of the session, they discuss anything special that is coming up, say good-bye, and go to their next class.

David and his Circle of Friends go on fun trips that Miss Wachter arranges. Two weeks before Christmas, David and 13 of his friends rode the city bus to the mall. The whole group had their picture taken with Santa, and then they ate lunch at a Mexican restaurant before going back to school.

David's middle school had a special program for the seventh-graders to help them get to know each other better and learn to work together. They went with their teachers to Camp Cheley. Everyone practiced survival skills, ran obstacle courses, took night walks, went hiking and mountain climbing, and walked on a high wire. All of these events were designed to teach the kids to cooperate as a team. David liked climbing Mt. Cathedral best because he was the first person in his group to make it to the top. He did well on the high wire, but when he was supposed to free-fall down, he got scared. David's team of kids got a ladder and helped him off the wire. Halfway down the ladder David stopped and said, "Thanks, guys!" and everyone cheered. David had lots of fun at Camp Cheley and hopes to go back someday.

David has a busy schedule just like any other seventh-grader. Besides school and homework, he plays basketball and soccer. David and his soccer team won the Pepsi Cup Championship in 1991 and had their picture in the paper. David started skiing when he was eight, and it is his favorite sport. In 1992, he

won a scholarship for free ski lessons. David has lots of fun with his Boy Scout troop. He has gone on many camping trips and likes cooking on a campfire, making s'mores, and listening to stories. His sash is filled with the badges he has earned for doing projects in first aid, physical fitness, science, and camping. He hopes to become an Eagle Scout one day.

IN DAVID'S OWN WORDS
(with help from a friend)

I feel very proud inside that someone cares enough to write about me. I feel so lucky! I bet this book will explain that there are hardly any differences between people without disabilities and people with them. I hope that after people read this book, they will start looking at people with different abilities in a new and nicer way.

David Billars
Tiger
CSA Spring 1990

QUESTIONS & ANSWERS ABOUT DOWN SYNDROME AND CIRCLE OF FRIENDS

When we wrote this chapter on David, we met his Circle of Friends. We were so impressed with what they do that we are including information on the Circle of Friends as well as on Down syndrome.

What causes Down syndrome?
Down syndrome is caused by a problem with chromosomes. Think of chromosomes as the blueprint of your body. They determine what you will look like when you grow up as well as many other characteristics. People with Down syndrome have one extra chromosome in every cell in their body. Here's what it is like. Let's say all the houses on a particular street have ten windows, but one has 11. The house with 11 windows is like a person with Down syndrome.

What are the symptoms of Down syndrome?
Babies with Down syndrome have weak muscles that make it hard for them to hold their heads up and swallow their food. Some have heart problems. A high number of people with Down syndrome have some degree of hearing loss. They get physical therapy to help develop their muscles, occupational therapy to learn life skills such as feeding themselves, and speech therapy to help them talk more clearly.

What is a person with Down syndrome like?
Boys and girls with Down syndrome each have their own personality. Some may be shy and others may be outgoing. They can be of any ethnic heritage and live in any part of the world.

What does someone with Down syndrome look like?
People with Down syndrome look a lot like you and me. There are only a few differences that you can see. They have shorter toes and fingers, and the palms of their hands may have deep creases. Their eyes are usually a little slanted, and their faces are a little flatter. Sometimes you can see these differences right at birth, sometimes not until they are young children.

What is life like for an adult with Down syndrome?
People with Down syndrome can leave home and get a job just like people without a disability. Most adults with Down syndrome take the bus since they don't usually drive. Some adults live alone or share an apartment. Others live in a group home with someone to help them. Many companies have special jobs for people with Down syndrome.

Why would I want to join a Circle of Friends?
The Circle of Friends gives you the opportunity to meet a lot of people and to help someone with special needs. For example, you could help your new

Working out on the ropes

friend be accepted in school and prevent others from teasing him or her. We think that kids with disabilities do not want us to feel sorry for them. They want to be treated like friends. Joining a Circle of Friends can help you to see the similarities between people with disabilities and people without disabilities. It can also help you learn how to treat everyone with respect and become a friendlier person. Being in a Circle of Friends shows people that you care for others, not just for yourself. It can make you feel good to know you are helping others.

Will I make new friends?

People who have disabilities like it when others notice them in a friendly way. They will be a friend to you if you are a friend to them. Friends need to trust each other, and sometimes this takes time.

Why does the person with a Circle of Friends need me?

People with disabilities sometimes need a helping hand or someone to stick up for them. Once you learn about people with disabilities, you can be a guide and help kids learn how to treat those with special needs with kindness.

How do I join a Circle of Friends?

Ask if your school, church, scout troop, or other group you belong to has a Circle of Friends. You could join a Circle of Friends by finding out who is in charge of it and talking to them about it. Or you could ask your parents or your teacher to help you start your own.

Our Poem Dedicated to David

> *The greatest disability is having
>   no friends,
> And this is one that we can bring
>   to an end.*

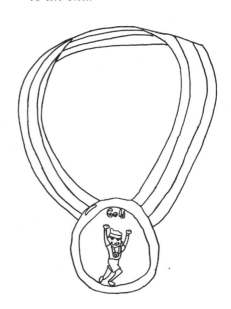

KELLY YOUNG
Living with Hemophilia

Live from the Twin Cities! It's the seventh game of the 1991 World Series! It's the bottom of the tenth inning. The bases are loaded with Gladden on third. Gene Larkin steps to the plate. The Braves pull the outfield in, and Gene Larkin gets a hit. Gladden scores, and the Minnesota Twins win their second World Series. Kelly and Dillon Young go wild!

Kelly and Dillon are triple twins. They live in the Twin Cities, they are Twins fans, and they are twin brothers. Kelly and Dillon do lots of things twins' style. They're double trouble playing basketball, kickball, and baseball. Kelly

and Dillon are the double dudes in dark blue in the fifth grade class at St. Jerome's school.

You might think same, same, same, but these twins are kind of different. If the twins are playing basketball and Kelly hurts himself, it could be double trouble. Kelly bleeds double time, and double Band-Aids just don't cut it.

Kelly has hemophilia *(hee-moh-FEE-lee-uh)*. Hemophilia is a blood disorder that makes it hard for a person to stop bleeding and form a scab. When clotting works properly, our blood thickens when we get hurt and forms a wall that stops the bleeding. The wall that

John Twohig

Kelly (right) and his twin brother, Dillon, answering questions for the fourth grade authors

Kelly's blood makes is like a brick wall with all of the cement missing. So the blood may keep pouring into a very small area like a joint or muscle. When Kelly gets a regular cut on his skin, it bleeds longer than normal but it's not really dangerous. What is most serious is when Kelly twists a joint or bruises a muscle. Then he bleeds inside and the joint or muscle fills up with blood. This is called a bleed. Imagine your knee filling up with blood under your skin. You wouldn't be able to bend it, and the swelling would be very painful.

Kelly's story starts before he was even born. The Youngs had a little boy named Brian who was two years old, and they wanted to have another baby. Finally, Mrs. Young got pregnant. She is a carrier for hemophilia because her father had it, so the doctor asked Mrs. Young to come in for an amniocentesis, a test to see if the baby is healthy. Although carriers don't actually have the disease themselves, they can pass hemophilia on to their sons through a gene.

During the test, the nurse's eyes suddenly got very big. Mrs. Young asked, "What's the matter?" The nurse told her they had to wait for the doctor. Mrs. Young said she had to know immediately what was wrong or she would jump off the table.

The nurse said, "I think there are two."

Mrs. Young gasped. "My baby has two heads?!"

The nurse said, "No, there are two babies!" Mrs. Young started laughing and talking loudly. Mr. Young and Brian ran in from the waiting room. The doctor told the Youngs it was riskier to do the amniocentesis on twins, so they decided to stop the test immediately. They didn't care if they had boys or girls or whether their babies had hemophilia or not. A geneticist, a person who studies genes and inherited traits, contacted Mrs. Young about continuing with the test. This person told Mrs. Young that she would not want to bring babies who were less than perfect into the world. Mr. and Mrs. Young believe you can't bring a baby who is less than perfect into the world, because all people are perfect in their own way.

On March 28, 1982, the twins were born seven weeks early. They are fraternal twins, not identical twins, so they do not look the same. Kelly weighed 5 pounds and 14 ounces, and Dillon weighed 6 pounds. Both of the boys had to be put in an incubator because their lungs weren't fully developed. (An incubator is a warm, enclosed crib that sends a steady flow of oxygen to the baby.)

Mr. and Mrs. Young had asked their doctor if he would check the twins and

John Twohig

Kelly and Dillon working on an art project with fifth grade classmates

John Twohig

Dillon and Kelly taking part in physical education class

let them know if either had hemophilia. Later, a person they didn't even know walked into Mrs. Young's room and told her that "Baby B" did in fact have hemophilia. Mrs. Young was shocked, but not because her baby had hemophilia. She thought it was awful that the person called Kelly "Baby B." Mrs. Young knew she would love both boys equally.

Kelly has a very severe case of hemophilia, and his medical care has been difficult at times. Before he was two he had been in the hospital 29 times. By the time he was ten, he had had seven major surgeries. In kindergarten Kelly had a lot of trouble with bleeds. Since bleeds often happen in the joints, Kelly had trouble walking, but he went to school anyway and used a wheelchair to get around.

Fortunately, he had a very good teacher named Mrs. Spoden. She realized how important it was for Kelly to take part, even when he was in his wheelchair. She made up games for him to play with the class. When Mrs. Spoden had gym class she had all the other kids run around Kelly and throw Nerf balls to him. Kelly would try to catch as many balls as possible, and everyone had a great time. Mrs. Spoden's work gave Kelly a great start at St. Jerome's, and each teacher has continued working hard to include him.

When Kelly was in second grade, he had a bad bleed by his kidney. He was put in a body cast from his chest to his ankles. He still came to school in his wheelchair, and all of his classmates worked to help him as much as possible.

When Kelly was in fourth grade, his port-a-cath got infected, and he had to be in the hospital for five weeks. A port-a-cath is a small round pad that is sewn under the skin. Kelly can poke a needle into the pad and send medication to his heart. While he was in the hospital he watched the Twins win the World Series. From his bed, Kelly cheered for his favorite player, Greg Gagne. The local television news team came and taped Kelly cheering for the Twins. They asked who his favorite player was, and he told them. Greg Gagne heard about Kelly and called him on the phone. He talked with Kelly and his family for about an hour. Kelly was so excited he could hardly talk. When Greg Gagne told Kelly good-bye he said, "I will be praying for you."

A week later Kelly received a special package. Inside was a photograph of Greg Gagne and a baseball, a handkerchief with the Twins' emblem on it, and an autographed baseball bat from the World Series. Kelly noticed that Mr. Gagne had printed John 3:16 next to his autograph. This is a scripture from the Bible that says, "For God so loved the world that He gave His only son so that everyone who believes in Him shall not die but have eternal life." Kelly and his

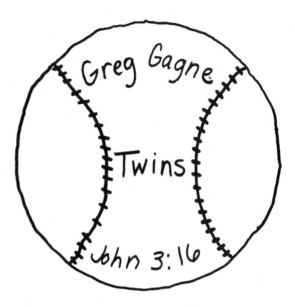

class at school memorized the verse and think that it is very special.

Even though Kelly has a very severe case of hemophilia, he is in good shape and can be very active. Many hemophiliacs' joints cannot bend because blood has filled up those areas so many times. Bleeds inside Kelly's joints and muscles are the thing that trouble him the most, and they must be treated. Kelly has learned how to treat himself.

About three times a month, Kelly gets a bleed that needs to be treated twice a day for two or three days. To treat himself, Kelly pumps Factor 8 into his veins. Factor 8 is a part of healthy blood that is missing from Kelly's blood. It helps blood clot and stops bleeding.

Kelly used to get the Factor 8 into his system by inserting an IV into a vein. An IV is a needle connected to a long, thin tube. The needle is placed into a vein, usually in an arm. Then the needle is pulled out, but the tube stays in so blood can be put into the body. Because Kelly's veins had been punctured with so many IV needles, it became extremely difficult to find one that could take an IV. In fact, once when Kelly was in the hospital, it took days before the doctors and nurses could get an IV started. They searched all over his body, even on his head, for a vein that could take an IV. The doctors finally decided that Kelly needed to have an operation to make his treatment less difficult.

The doctors connected a small, long tube called a Hickman to Kelly's heart. The tube comes out of his chest, and Kelly now uses it to get the Factor 8 into his body. He doesn't have to poke himself with needles any more, but treating himself is still tough. He needs to flush the tube of the Hickman with a special cleaning solution every day to keep it clean and open. The Hickman helps Kelly lead a more regular life, but if it ever begins to cause an infection, it might be replaced by a port-a-cath.

There is no cure for hemophilia, so Kelly will need these treatments all his life. Most hemophiliacs Kelly's age don't treat themselves. Even an LPN (Licensed Practical Nurse) at the hospital can't do some of the things Kelly does. Wow! LPNs go to school for years, and Kelly is only in fifth grade. Kelly has his mom to

John Twohig

Kelly playing baseball

thank for this. She taught him how to treat himself. In fact, she became so good at treating Kelly that with her family's encouragement, she became a nurse.

Kelly has many helpers. A whole team of doctors work together to make Kelly's treatment easier. His doctors and nurses are always surprised at how well Kelly and his family are controlling his hemophilia. They work very hard to treat Kelly, and they never give up. Dr. Jack Priest, Dr. Chris Moertel and Dr. Jim McCord are so important in Kelly's life that they are almost like part of the family. When Kelly goes to the dentist, one of his doctors has to make special arrangements because if his mouth starts bleeding it might not stop. If Kelly wants to take something for a headache or a runny nose, he has to call one of his doctors, because the medication could affect his bleeding.

A friend Mrs. Young worked with, Ms. Taylor, also helps Kelly in a very special way. She donates blood for him. Once a month, she goes to a blood bank, and the staff there takes out some of her blood. It takes about five hours. Ms. Taylor is a nurse and a busy single mom, but she still takes time to donate blood. This is very important to Kelly, because he needs a steady supply of healthy blood.

Kelly and his twin brother, Dillon, have a very close relationship. They have always been in the same class, and when they get in trouble at school they try to blackmail one another. They try to get something from the other one for promising not to tattle. If Kelly gets in trouble, Dillon asks for basketball cards. When Dillon is the one in trouble, Kelly says a Troll for his collection will keep him quiet. But once he has the Troll, he may be sneaky and tell on Dillon anyway!

Although Kelly and Dillon do many things together, there are some places that Kelly goes without Dillon. One of these places is Camp Courage. There he spends one fun-filled week making crafts, swimming, canoeing, fishing, sleeping in cabins, eating good food, playing pranks, and having a wonderful time. There is a big lake where the kids play water volleyball and have water fights. At night, they listen to ghost stories around the campfire. When it's time to go to sleep, everyone shares cabins. Sometimes they play tricks on one other, like teepeeing the other cabins or putting whipped cream in someone's bed!

At school Kelly is the only kid with hemophilia, but at Camp Courage all the kids have it. These kids have all spent a lot of time around medical stuff, so they do things a little differently. When they have water fights, for example, instead of using balloons and squirt guns, they use surgical gloves and syringes. At Camp Courage the counselors have to be very careful about what they say and do. When the kids learn how to put in the sharp IV needles, they practice on their counselors!

One day Mr. and Mrs. Young were contacted by a support group for parents of children with hemophilia. They asked if Kelly would come talk to their group. He agreed to talk to the group.

Even though he was nervous, he got up in front of them and answered all the questions the parents had. One parent asked Kelly if he was sad that he had hemophilia. Kelly just said, "Why?" He didn't know why someone would think he would be sad about his way of life. He enjoys life so much.

Mr. and Mrs. Young value life, and their sons are the most important people in the world to them. Kelly has it a little tougher than a lot of kids, but that doesn't stop him. He wants to be the first hemophiliac to win the gold medal for swimming in the Olympics. Kelly is a strong person and has so much to share and give. His attitude about life can teach us all a lot.

IN KELLY'S OWN WORDS

I know what I can do, so don't hold me back. If something is dangerous for me, I won't do it. I know when I need to slow down. Otherwise, I give it all I've got. I don't even think of myself as having special needs. My Hickman and injections are just a part of me.

It's easy to treat myself. I learned quickly what injections to take, and when and how to inject them. It's taken longer to know when I need to treat myself, but now I have that down for the most part. So just treat me like anyone else.

QUESTIONS & ANSWERS ABOUT HEMOPHILIA

We have learned lots of information about hemophilia. Here are some facts we thought you would like to know.

What is hemophilia?
Hemophilia is a blood disorder that makes it hard for a person to stop bleeding. We all have 13 factors in our blood, little parts that each play a part in circulation and clotting. People with hemophilia don't have as much of one factor, usually Factor 8. Factor 8 helps your blood form a clot and stops the bleeding when you are injured inside. When a hemophiliac bleeds inside, it takes a lot longer for the bleeding to stop because his blood doesn't have enough Factor 8.

How do you get hemophilia?
You can't catch hemophilia the way you can catch a cold or the chicken pox. Hemophilia is inherited through the genes. People are born with it.

How are kids with hemophilia affected?
Kids with hemophilia can do almost everything everyone else can do. People with hemophilia may be able to play most sports. They may play football and baseball and swim in the summer. There might be a kid in your school who has hemophilia, and you don't even know it because he looks and acts like everyone else. However, kids with hemophilia do have to be more careful when they do certain things, especially if there's a danger of cutting, bumping, or hurting themselves. If they hurt themselves they could develop a bleed.

Why are most hemophiliacs boys?
The hemophilia gene can be passed through a woman carrier to her sons, so mostly boys have it. But girls can be carriers of hemophilia. If Kelly had a sister there would be a 50/50 chance she would be a carrier of hemophilia but not a hemophiliac herself. But if a woman who carries hemophilia married a man with hemophilia, and they had a daughter, she could get hemophilia. This is very rare.

Kelly playing kickball with his author friends

Why did Kelly get hemophilia, but his twin brother Dillon didn't?

Kelly and Dillon are fraternal twins, so they each got different genes. (Identical twins get the same genes.) Kelly got the blood gene that causes hemophilia but Dillon didn't. Girls' chromosomes are called XX. Boys' are called XY. A woman who is a carrier of hemophilia has an X with a little difference. We show this with an *X. In Kelly's family, the genes look like this:

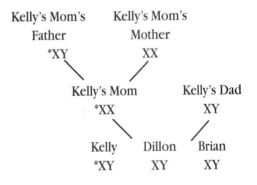

Kelly got the *X with the little difference. Brian and Dillon didn't.

Our Poem Dedicated to Kelly

You would like Kelly Young to be in your class.
He loves sports, the Twins, and he serves at Mass.
He treats himself when he gets a bleed.
His kind of spirit we all need.

GENA PERRY
Living with a Hearing Impairment

Gena felt like the happiest person in the world. She was about to give her first riding lesson at Praying Hands Ranch, a camp for children with disabilities. She couldn't wait to find out who was going to ride her favorite horse, Beauty. She paused for a moment to look at the beautiful Rocky Mountains. A gentle breeze was blowing, carrying the sweet smell of prairie flowers.

Around the corner came a woman and, skipping beside her, a little girl with her hair in a pony tail. Gena went to introduce herself to them. Seven-year-old Lauren was excited because she was going to ride a horse for the very first time. Lauren's mom asked Gena to be careful in helping Lauren because she was just learning to read lips and might have trouble understanding Gena. Gena laughed and said, "We'll get along just fine. I'm hearing impaired too."

Gena Perry, a bouncy 15-year-old, has accomplished many things. She is very outgoing and talks clearly. She showed us her courage by standing up in front of our whole class and telling us about her life. She has won awards for writing, running, photography, good grades, and sports. She is a wonderful, cheerful person who loves to have fun.

Gena at home with her two sisters, Michaela and Brianna

Christie Logsdon

When Gena was born, she had a heart problem. When she was eight months old, she had open heart surgery to fix the problem. Her parents became worried because Gena was not babbling like most babies do at that age. Her mom didn't understand why Gena didn't even try to talk. Even when her dad stomped up and down the stairs, Gena didn't seem to notice. When her mom called her name to get her attention or wake her up, Gena would not respond. The Perrys talked to Gena's doctor, but he said he wasn't worried. He told them that they just expected too much because they were teachers. The

doctor believed Gena would start to talk if they gave her time.

But at 1½ years old Gena still wasn't talking. When she was two years old, the Perrys decided to make an appointment with an ear doctor. Dr. Perry, Gena's mom, took her for her first hearing test. The doctor explained Gena's problem. He said Gena had a profound hearing loss. She couldn't hear a thing—not even a really loud fire alarm—without strong hearing aids.

Gena's parents thought about what they should do. Should Gena learn sign language or use hearing aids and learn to speak? Her parents were determined

Christie Logsdon

Gena and her dog

that she should have every chance to be all she was intended to be, so they enrolled her in a special clinic to learn to speak aloud. When Gena got her first hearing aids, her whole face lit up. She could finally hear sounds. Her mom was so happy she cried. Unlike most kids, Gena's first words were "woof-woof." But her very next words were "mama" and "dada."

When Gena was three years old, she had an operation on her ears. Gena told us it felt like the doctor had cut off her ears. He had to look inside to see if he could do anything to make her hear better. The doctor had tried his best, but there was nothing he could do to improve Gena's hearing.

Gena went to a regular elementary school because her parents wanted her to learn to speak and to read lips. To help her learn to read lips, Gena's teacher wore a microphone, and Gena used a receiver that amplified what the teacher said. It was like her teacher was a disc jockey at a radio station and Gena was the audience. Gena doesn't use this system as much anymore because she has learned to read lips so well.

Gena has a great family who loves her deeply. She is the oldest of four kids. Michaela is nine, Brianna is seven, and Josiah is four. We are lucky that Gena's sister Michaela is in our class, so we got to write this chapter about Gena.

Gena's dad is a fifth grade teacher. He also works at the Denver Zoo's nursery every other Saturday. Gena's mom is a school principal. The family enjoys doing things together and often visits the zoo. They go to church every Sunday and take neat family trips. On one trip they went to Disneyland. Two of Gena's favorite rides were "It's A Small World" and "Space Mountain." Gena got her picture taken with Mickey Mouse. The Perrys also enjoy going to Denver Nuggets and Colorado Rockies games together.

One of Gena's favorite stories is about running in the 1991 Bolder Boulder, a 10K Memorial Day race. She and her dad were waiting for the gun to go off. Although Gena couldn't hear the gun, she saw the starter say "go," and she took off with her dad and the crowd. During the race, Gena slowed down. Her dad thought she was tired and slowed down, too. When Gena realized she had psyched her dad out, she took off and left him behind. Gena crossed the finish line 17th out of the 111 kids in her age group. She was waiting at the finish when her dad finally crossed the line. Gena and her dad joked all the way home about that year's race. Now it's a tradition for them to run the race together each year.

Sometimes, Gena and her mom go shopping together at the mall. Gena likes to use her babysitting money to treat her mom to lunch. Gena and her mom like to do many things together. They are planting a garden in their back-

yard. They like to keep in shape by doing step aerobics and sit-ups.

Gena's dad drives her to speech therapy on Wednesday. Gena's teacher, Mrs. Ernst, tries to help Gena listen better instead of only reading lips. She even covers her mouth with her hand, and Gena must listen to figure out what she is saying. They work very hard on pronouncing words. The teacher has Gena touch her throat so she can feel the vocal chords vibrate in different ways as each word is said. Sometimes Gena has to do homework. Most of the time she does the homework by herself, but sometimes her parents help her. She told us that her therapy can be boring,

Christie Logsdon

Gena (right) with her friend Christy

but she still goes because she wants to learn to speak even better.

Gena wears her hearing aids when she is awake to help her hear as much sound as possible. She takes them out when she goes to bed. Since she cannot hear an alarm clock without her hearing aids, she has a special machine called a Shake Awake. It looks like an alarm clock, but it shakes instead of rings. Gena puts it under her pillow, and it shakes the pillow at the time she sets it to go off. The first time she used it, it shook the whole bed and scared her! Now she appreciates the Shake Awake because she needs to be at school by 7:30.

Since Gena cannot hear someone talk to her on the phone, she has a special Telecommunications Device for the Deaf (TDD). A TDD has a keyboard and a small screen. When she wants to talk to someone over the phone, she first calls the Colorado Relay Service. Then she types in the number and the name of the person she wants to call. The relay service calls that person and asks if he or she can take the call. If the person says yes, the relay service types what the person is saying so Gena can read the words on her screen. Gena can then type or say aloud whatever she wants to say to the person.

Since Gena enjoys children and likes making money, she babysits almost every weekend. Gena likes to buy clothes and the CDs of Amy Grant and Tom Petty. Gena also likes to cook Chinese food, Mexican food, and macaroni and cheese for the kids she babysits. When she takes care of Kevin and Kyle, she has fun telling them stories that she makes up. Gena loves karate and so do the boys, so she tells them stories about heroes who use karate to save themselves.

Gena has a big dream. When she grows up she wants to teach children about the stars (astronomy). We all think she would make a great teacher because she is peppy and smart, energetic and cheerful. Gena knows that she can do anything if she tries. Because Gena is six years older than we are, she could graduate from college when we are in high school. In fact, if her dream comes true, she may be our science teacher someday.

IN GENA'S OWN WORDS

Would you like to get to know me better? I would like to get better acquainted with you, too! It's easy to do—just talk to me. I have noticed that sometimes people are afraid to talk to me because they know that I am hearing impaired. They are worried that I won't understand them. Don't worry, if I don't understand something you say, I will ask you about it.

It helps if you stand where I can see your face (it's hard to read your lips when all I can see is the back of your head!). Also, if you stand with the sun or a bright light behind your head,

Christie Logsdon

Gena talking with the young authors who wrote this chapter

sometimes shadows get on your face and it is hard to see your mouth. You don't need to talk really slow or really loud. Especially, please don't exaggerate how you enunciate each word. All those things distort the words you are saying. Remember, I am used to reading lips just the way people really talk, so that is what is easiest for me to lip read.

Because I am hearing impaired, people often wonder if I can talk. Believe me, I can! In fact, sometimes my dad says I talk too much! My voice sounds a little different though. My friends say it sounds like I have a foreign accent. If you don't understand what I say, it's no big deal. Just ask me. But please include me in your conversation.

Christie Logsdon

Gena answering students' questions

Sometimes when everybody is talking at once, I won't be able to lip read it all, and I will have to ask you what was said. *Please* don't say, "I'll tell you later," and then forget to do it. That drives me crazy! More than anything, just treat me like you would treat any other friend. I'd love to be friends with you.

QUESTIONS & ANSWERS ABOUT HEARING IMPAIRMENT

We found out many things about being hearing impaired by asking questions.

What does it mean to be hearing impaired?

Some people believe that "hearing impaired" and "deaf" mean the same thing. Other people told us that when you are deaf you can't hear anything, but if you are hearing impaired you can hear something, although it might sound like just a whisper. In our book we have chosen to use the term hearing impaired because that is how Gena refers to herself.

Some people who are hearing impaired cannot understand spoken conversation without the help of a hearing aid. They may hear some sounds without the hearing aid, but these sounds are too faint to be understood.

There are many types and degrees of hearing loss. Try plugging your ears and having a friend whisper something to you. What you hear is kind of what it's like to have a hearing loss.

Christie Logsdon

Gena doing her homework

With other types of hearing loss, you can't hear certain frequencies. You might not hear the high tones of sounds or you might not hear the low tones. For example, you wouldn't hear all the notes of a song. Or in a conversation, you would hear silences where the tones you couldn't hear should be.

How do you become hearing impaired?

You can become hearing impaired from many different things. Most commonly people are born with a hearing impairment. If a baby has a lot of ear infections, he or she might get a hearing impairment. A person might become hearing impaired by listening to very loud music or going to a rock concert and sitting too close to the loud speaker. Adults might get a hearing loss from operating noisy machines every day at their jobs. Many people lose their hearing naturally from old age.

How long does it take to tell that a person is hearing impaired?

A person can be tested for a hearing loss in a short amount of time. If a baby is not learning to speak, does not react to loud noises, or doesn't seem to notice when someone calls his or her name, it might be a sign of hearing loss. Adults might find out later in life that they lost some of their hearing and not even know when it happened.

Do hearing impaired people ever get their hearing back?

Hearing impaired people usually do not get their hearing back and are hearing impaired their whole lives. There are some things that can be done to help hearing impaired people hear a little better. They might have surgery, or they might wear hearing aids to help make the sounds louder in their ears.

Can hearing impaired people talk?

Hearing impaired people can talk, but it takes a lot of work to learn how. Imagine trying to learn another language without ever being able to hear someone say the words correctly. Hearing impaired people that do talk sound a little different from people who can hear. Some people sound like they have foreign accents, and some exaggerate the sounds in words. Many hearing impaired people spend a lot of time with voice therapists who help them learn to speak by watching and touching. A hearing impaired person can feel how words are sounded by touching their teacher's throat or their own throat while they talk. Some hearing impaired people choose not to talk and prefer to use sign language or another form of communication.

What is sign language?

Sign language is a language made up of hand movements, gestures, and facial expressions. Each letter of the alphabet is signed in a different way. Just as Spanish and Japanese are complete languages, American Sign Language (ASL) is a language in itself, with thousands of signs for different words. There are many places where you can take a class and learn sign language. Check in your phone book under "Deaf" or "Hearing Impaired" to see what organizations are in your area.

How do you talk to hearing impaired people?

If they can read lips, you talk to hearing impaired people just as you would to a hearing person. If the person cannot read lips, then you could spell out what you want to say using hand signs, act out what you want to say, learn American Sign Language, or write a note.

What are some of the things that make life easier for hearing impaired people?

There are many things that help hearing impaired people. In this chapter, you learned about the Shake Awake and the Telecommunications Device for the Deaf (TDD). Many hearing impaired people have doorbells that flash a light instead of ringing when someone is at the door. There are also phones that flash a light when the phone rings, and alarm clocks that light up instead of make noise.

To watch television, hearing impaired people use a system called closed captioning. A program that is closed captioned runs a special symbol

on the screen to tell hearing impaired people they can use close captions. A special box called a decoder box prints the words spoken on the show at the bottom of the TV screen. This way a hearing impaired person can watch the show and read the words as they are spoken. We found out that as of 1993, new televisions have this decoder box built right inside the television. In fact, if you have a newer television, you could try this to see what it is like.

Our Poem Dedicated to Gena

*Gena is loving and caring in
    every way,*
*Her smile brightens each and
    every day,*
*She may be hearing impaired but
    that doesn't matter,*
*She is full of life and she likes to
    chatter!*

JOE KOVACH
Living with Blindness

It was a bright spring morning. A tall, dark-haired young man hurried along the sidewalk. He waited at the busy street while buses, trucks, and cars passed during the morning rush hour. He was near the end of his ten-block walk to Englewood High School and was worried about being late for class. He was thinking about his unfinished ceramics project. When the traffic stopped, he went across the street, up the school steps, and down the hall. He got to his classroom as the tardy bell rang.

Joe Kovach thought of ceramics as his "blast class" because it was an easy A.

During the 50-minute period, he had to complete a mold for his latest project. His classmates were doubtful he could do it, but Joe was sure. He showed them! At the end of the period, Joe's mold of the Eiffel Tower stood proud and tall. Joe's classmates congratulated him as he walked down the crowded hallway toward World History class.

Joe was thinking about the test he would be taking on World War II. As other students got out their pencils and paper, Joe took out his Braille machine and prepared for the test. Because Joe is blind, his teacher had the school Braillist translate the test into Braille for Joe

Joe demonstrating how you write using a Braille machine

Lori Stober

to read. Braille is a set of dots raised on paper that blind people read with their finger tips. After Joe finished the test, his answers were translated from Braille back to the regular alphabet so his teacher could grade it.

Even though Joe is blind, he takes a full load of seven subjects in school. His favorite class is algebra. You might think it would be hard to understand algebra if you couldn't see the symbols, but Joe doesn't. He thinks algebra is very interesting. Sometimes he shows his sense of humor by cupping his hands over his mouth and saying, "Teach, remember to read the board." The teacher laughs and reads the board for Joe so he can understand the problems.

At lunchtime Joe eats in the cafeteria. He can carry his lunch tray to a table without any trouble. He usually sits at the same table, which is located near the door so he can leave the room easily.

Joe uses a walking stick to get around school. His stick is longer than most walking sticks because he takes long steps. Sometimes he bumps into things and people with it, but most people don't care.

Joe's story began when he was born three months premature on September 30, 1976. He was so tiny that the doctors didn't think he would live. He weighed 1 pound and 13 ounces and was only 14 inches long. Joe was placed on a warming table under a heat lamp to help keep him alive. Because he wasn't breathing right, he was put on a breathing ventilator. The doctors had to give him a lot of oxygen and this hurt his eyes. His left eye went completely blind, and he lost all but 40 percent of his vision in his right eye.

Joe's preschool years were like anyone else's. Even though he couldn't see much, he still got around well. He played in the yard, rode his bike, and liked to be outside.

When Joe started kindergarten, his teacher and his family had a big decision to make. Should Joe use the regular alphabet in large print or should he learn Braille, since one day he might go blind? Everyone decided Joe should learn to read and write the regular alphabet.

Joe's life was mostly normal until the day before Easter in 1984, when Joe was a second grader. He woke up excited to color eggs. Joe and his five-year-old sister had just finished dying the Easter eggs when Joe's eyes began to feel blurry. He screamed, "Mom, something is wrong with my eyes! I can hardly see anything!" Joe was very scared. His mom took him to the hospital, and his eye doctor examined him. The retina had come loose in his good eye. The retina, located in the back of the eyeball, is a very important part of the eye. The doctor said Joe needed surgery. The

operation fixed the retina, but Joe still had a lot of fluid on his eye, and his sight was almost gone. His doctors in Denver decided Joe should see an eye surgeon in Boston who knew more about problems like Joe's.

When Joe and his mother got to Boston, Joe had to be in the hospital again. He had two more surgeries, but they didn't help. He was still almost completely blind. The doctors couldn't do anything more to help.

After Joe's operations, all he could see was lightness, darkness, shadows, and some movement. Even so, he could still enjoy many activities, like watching TV. Joe returned to Colorado to start third grade. The school district did not prepare his teachers for a blind student, so he was sent home for a while. His time at home gave him the chance to start mobility training. That means he was learning to move around by him-

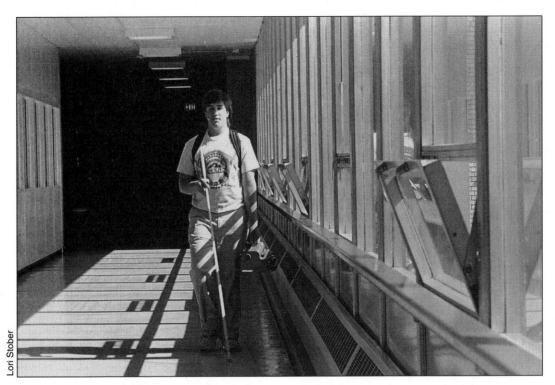

Joe using his walking stick

Lori Stober

self. Joe was taught how to use a walking stick by Pat Lewis, a teacher who helps visually impaired people. Mrs. Lewis was very important to Joe because she convinced him he could still get around and did not allow him to feel sorry for himself. Joe was amazed by how well Mrs. Lewis understood him even though she was not blind herself.

Joe soon started back into third grade at his school. One year later, Joe and his classmates were featured in a local newspaper. The article told all about his fourth-grade year. It showed how Joe was just one of the kids sitting in his classroom of happy fourth-graders. It told how Joe enjoyed playing football, liked Bruce Springsteen, and didn't like to clean his room. The article also shared how Joe's fourth grade teacher had his classmates put on a blindfold and take trust walks. This is when you pick a friend to lead you around and direct you to do things while you're blindfolded. They tried to brush their teeth blindfolded and also experimented with reading Braille. All of his classmates watched out for Joe in their own special way.

Joe moved to a suburb of Denver, Colorado, when he was going into seventh grade. His mobility teacher came to work with him again so he could learn to handle walking by himself in heavy city traffic.

Joe's vision didn't change again until he was in ninth grade. One day when he was watching television, the picture just started to fade away. In fact, it looked like the TV was moving backward. After a few minutes, Joe couldn't see anything but blackness. Today, he can open and close his eyelids but he doesn't see anything at all. Joe has continued to learn to handle his disability, and he says it is just the way it is.

Joe has lots of hobbies. He takes part in a Civil War club that keeps history alive. One weekend he went to a park with his club for a reenactment of a Civil War hospital. The hospital was open for 36 hours. Joe said he didn't get any sleep during the night. He was a guard and a patient. He saw the hospital through his fingertips.

Besides being a history fan, Joe enjoys playing games. One of his favorite board games is chess. He is very good at chess, and he tells the pieces apart by feeling them. Joe also plays Dungeons and Dragons, a role-playing game that requires a lot of imagination, time, and skill. Joe is good at this because he often pictures things in his mind.

Joe is in an organization that is very important to him. It is an International Masonic organization for young men, called Demolay, that helps others. They meet twice a month to discuss activities such as dances and the upcoming basketball tournament. He recently served at a pancake breakfast to help raise money for his chapter. Joe is now a junior deacon, and he is running for junior counselor. Someday he would like to be a Master Counselor, the leader of the organization.

Joe likes to "rock out" to music. He taught himself how to play the piano when he was young, and he has also tried playing the guitar and the drums. And Joe still likes to watch TV. He "watches" with his ears and creates images in his mind.

Joe loves sports. He remembers playing football in elementary school when he could see only shadows. He also remembers a field day when he participated in the 25-yard dash. To run in this event he needed a guide. When the gun went off, the guide led Joe down the field. With the guide's help, Joe was able to win a blue ribbon. Over the years, Joe's mom has encouraged him to try new and exciting things. Joe tried karate for a few lessons but decided it

wasn't for him. His mom is willing to help him work on most things, but she had put her foot down on one thing. She won't let him play football because she doesn't want him to get hurt.

One of Joe's favorite activities at school is wrestling. When Joe is in a match, he goes to the center of the mat and gets in the starting position. The referee blows the whistle. Joe, without seeing his opponent, moves around the mat, trying to pin the other wrestler. Even when Joe loses, he's not discouraged. You will find Joe lifting weights every day at Englewood High School, preparing for next year's wrestling season.

Lori Stober

Joe lifting weights on the overhead press

Joe is a very determined person and he never gives up. He believes he is blind for a reason, just like you are sighted for a reason. He feels that he may be famous one day. Who knows? When your children are reading their history books, they may learn about General Joe Kovach, a great military man who was blind, or about the first blind president of the United States.

IN JOE'S OWN WORDS

I want to be living proof that blind people can succeed. I have shared my story with you to help break down stereotypes of people who are blind. I want you to know you shouldn't overreact when you see someone who is blind,

Lori Stober

Joe in training for wrestling

but just treat them like anyone else. If you want to help someone, always ask them first. I believe that my family has helped me face my problem and encouraged me to be the best I can. I have learned to deal with my blindness. I have learned about the Americans with Disabilities Act that protects my rights. I feel that all disabled people need to study this and learn their rights.

QUESTIONS & ANSWERS ABOUT BLINDNESS

We learned a lot by asking Joe and others about blindness. Here are some of the things we found out.

What causes blindness?
People can become blind from many different things. When babies are born too early, they must be given a lot of oxygen. Sometimes this can cause blindness. That is what happened to Joe. If a pregnant woman gets sick with German measles, her child might be born blind. Injuries to the head, especially the back of the head, can cause blindness. Adults who have accidents at work with chemicals or fire can become blind, too.

Can blind people ever get their sight back?
A small number of blind people have their sight restored through surgery. The surgeon replaces the damaged part of their eyes with a healthy part given by a donor who has died. This is called transplant surgery.

How do blind people communicate?

Blind people talk just like you and me. Many blind people read an alphabet called Braille.

What is Braille?

Braille is a method of reading by touch. In Braille, every letter and number is represented by different arrangements of six dots that are raised on paper so the person can feel them. Many blind people read Braille just as fast as sighted people read print. Maybe you've seen Braille numbers in elevators on the floor button panel. Some restaurants have Braille menus.

How do dogs help blind people?

Some blind people use a guide dog to help them do things. Guide dogs are often called seeing eye dogs. They begin their training when they are puppies. The dog will help its master cross streets, go shopping, get around their house, and go through the day's routine. A national law allows guide dogs to go with their blind person inside restaurants, grocery stores, movies, planes, buses, or anyplace else. Guide dogs are also trained to protect their masters. Always ask before you pet or feed a guide dog.

How can you help a blind person?

If you see a blind person who seems to need some help, you should ask if they would like help instead of just grabbing his or her arm. The best way that you can help a blind person is to be a good friend to them. Not all blind people look or act like they are blind. Don't tease a blind person or tell them you think they are pretending to be blind. Some blind people's eyes look just like yours. One person told us that sometimes others don't believe she is blind, and they treat her poorly.

How does a blind person use a walking stick?

A trained counselor fits a blind person with a white walking stick made specially for the way they walk and for their height. Only people who are legally blind or in a training program can use the white stick. The blind person gently swings the walking stick back and forth in an arc, tapping the ground from side to side to feel for obstacles.

What does it mean to be legally blind?

A person is legally blind when he or she can only see at 20 feet what a person with normal vision can see at 200 feet. People with tunnel vision who cannot see to the side are also considered legally blind. People who are legally blind have special rights, and only they can use a white walking stick. Drivers must always give them the right of way.

Can blind people see anything?

There are many degrees of blindness. Some people who are blind may see only shadows. Some people can see light and dark, and others can see some colors. Some blind people can see nothing at all.

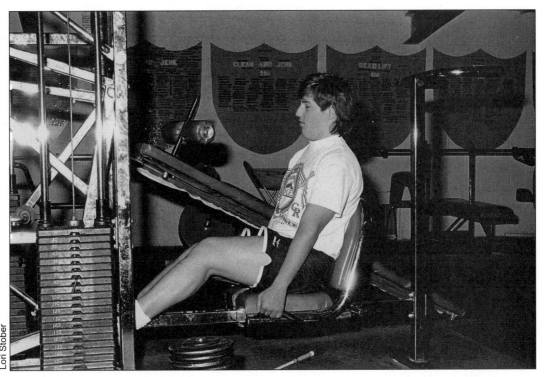

Lori Stober

Joe using the leg press

What kind of special tools or machines help people who are blind?

Besides Braille, Braille machines, guide dogs, and walking sticks, blind people can use talking calculators, talking computers, and even talking watches. A very helpful machine called a book scanner can read aloud whatever it scans on a page. Every day engineers and inventors are making things to help blind people.

Our Poem Dedicated to Joe

Although Joe cannot see,
Only his eyes are blind,
Because he sees a rainbow of
  colors,
All inside his mind.

AMY ALLEN
Living with Dwarfism

A small white Toyota Tercel pulls up to the curb, playing the latest Elton John tape. The driver hops out of the car. The children nearby stop in their tracks and stare at the driver. She is a pretty blonde girl who, to their surprise, is only 3'11", about the size of a third-grader.

The girl approaches the kids and asks, "Are you surprised I drove this car? I'm old enough to drive. I'm just short because I am a dwarf." This is how Amy Allen explains her disability to others. It's something she doesn't mind sharing.

Amy likes others to be educated about dwarfs. "Dwarf" is a medical term used to describe a person who will not grow normally due to bone or hormone problems. Amy's body is adult-sized, but her arms and legs are very short and stubby. Some dwarfs have other physical problems. Amy can't carry much weight because she has problems in her hips and legs. Amy wants both children and adults to ask questions about her disability, and not just wonder or be curious.

Amy likes to joke about being short. Her sense of humor makes it easier for others to accept her. After talking to Amy for a little while, her beautiful face, bright smile, and sparkling personality are all you notice. Amy is in a special class for

Anthony Allen

Amy (right) and her friend Maia in front of George Washington High School

very bright kids. She is a talented musician and a leader in her school. She is active in her community and her church. She may be small, but she is mighty!

Amy is a sophomore at George Washington High School. On a typical day at school, you might see Amy taking the elevator to get to a class. She uses a crutch to help her walk down the long halls. The crutch helps her with balance and gives her support for her hips. She jokes that her crutch could come in handy if she ever needs a weapon to protect herself!

Amy is in an accelerated program to prepare her for college. This program is called International Baccalaureate (*bak-uh-LOR-ee-ut*). About 600 high school students from all over Denver applied to be in this special program. Amy is one of eighty who qualified and is the only one with a disability. Because Amy is in an accelerated class, she has lots of homework and many big and heavy books. Amy can't carry all the books through the whole school day, so the school gave her two sets. One set of books is left at home to use for homework, and the other set stays at school.

Amy is talented in many subjects. She has studied French for three years and can speak it quite well. She is

Catholic and used her second language when she hosted French students during the World Youth Conference when the Pope came to Denver.

Amy's life began on September 23, 1976. She was the beautiful, blue-eyed baby girl born to Charles and Sally Allen. Amy was welcomed joyfully by her parents and her two-year-old brother. Her parents soon realized something about Amy was different. Her legs curved, and she didn't try to crawl. Amy didn't walk until she was two years old. In fact, Amy could talk before she could walk.

Amy's parents discussed her problems with a number of doctors, but they used medical terms that were hard to understand and didn't diagnose her problem. For many years, Amy wore leg braces from her hips down to her feet. In kindergarten and elementary school,

Amy's teachers helped the other students understand her disability by having her take the braces off so the other children could try them on. They were able to see how the braces worked and what it felt like to wear them. Amy's sense of humor made the class feel comfortable with her disability, and it made her feel better, too. In the meantime, her parents continued to talk to more doctors and read as many medical books as they could.

When Amy was eight, the doctors discovered Amy would be a dwarf, never taller than a third- or fourth-grader. This was sad for Amy and hard for her parents. They worried about what Amy's life would be like.

The Allens found support through a group called Little People of America (LPA). This is a nationwide organization that provides friendship and support for little people and their families. In this group the Allens could talk to other people about their feelings, and find out new information about dwarfism. They met all kinds of different families. In some families, the parents were little people and the kids were average-sized. In other families, one parent was a dwarf and the other was average-sized. Some families had only dwarf children, and other families had both sizes. Through support groups such as the LPA, the Allens decided they should not let a disability stop Amy from doing anything she set her mind to do.

When Amy turned 16, Mr. Allen used his engineering skills to extend the

Anthony Allen

Amy's father extended the brake and gas pedals on Amy's car

gas and brake pedals on Amy's car so she could drive. Amy sits on a pillow so she can reach the steering wheel. Driving is a lot of fun for Amy, just like it is for anyone else.

Mrs. Allen does lots of things to help Amy, too. Besides shortening all of Amy's clothes, Mrs. Allen has taken lots of classes to learn Amy's rights guaranteed by the Americans with Disabilities Act. During middle school, Amy had surgery to insert metal plates in her legs to help keep them straight. She was in a body cast for almost two months. All of her mother's classes paid off because she knew Amy was entitled by law to have a

tutor at home. Even though the school didn't want to give her a tutor, Amy's mother fought for her rights and won. Amy was able to keep learning at home.

Amy laughs when you ask her about her brother Anthony because their personalities are opposite. Although they are very different, Amy and Anthony watch out for each other. Anthony is never embarrassed to help his sister. When they go to an amusement park, he helps Amy get on the rides. He also gives her advice about boyfriends. It is funny to see Amy and Anthony fight and tease each other because Anthony is two feet taller than Amy.

Amy's best friend is Maia *(MAY-ah)* Benjamin-Wardle. Maia is a pretty, dark-haired, browned-eyed, average-sized girl. Maia and Amy enjoy spending their free time together. They like to shop, eat out, go to concerts, and attend each other's special events.

Amy's interests do not stop with her studies. She has a sparkle in her eye when she talks about her music because she really wants to be a famous musician. Amy's family has always loved music. Her grandparents often take the whole family to hear the symphony. They also have season tickets to a nearby performing arts center. She likes to go to plays and concerts with them. One time Amy and her grandfather had a special date to see Eddie Daniels, Amy's favorite clarinet player.

Amy can play the saxophone, the oboe, and the piano, but her real love is for the clarinet. Amy began playing the clarinet when she was in fifth grade. She soon realized she needed to have her clarinet changed to help her play. The thumb rest was moved to make it easier for her short fingers to reach the keys.

Amy remembers when her fifth-grade music teacher said to her, "You will never be able to play because your hands are too small." Amy never believed what he told her. She has a special dream that someday she will play in the London Symphony. Amy practices 15 to 20 hours every week to make her dream come true. She hopes her grandfather will be in the front row of the audience, smiling proudly at her.

Amy plays in her school band and in special groups, and she takes private clarinet lessons. She also pays for a weekly half-hour lesson, but her teacher, Chuck Schneider, usually keeps her for an hour or more because he believes she will be a big hit someday. We believe Amy Allen will make her dream come true, and one day we will buy one of her CDs.

IN AMY'S OWN WORDS

If there is one thing that I would like people to know, it is that people with disabilities are people, too. Just because we are not like everyone else on the outside does not mean that we do not have feelings on the inside. Just like other people, disabled people have dreams for the future and places we want to go. Disabled people want to have friends like everyone else, and it does not matter if they are disabled, too—not everyone's friends are the same! There is one thing that I would like to ask everyone. Just treat disabled people as you treat everyone else. We are not that different from you.

Amy works with a partner on a class project

QUESTIONS & ANSWERS ABOUT DWARFISM

Here are some questions and answers about dwarfs that we thought might interest you.

What is a dwarf?

The word "dwarf" is a medical term. A dwarf has a regular-sized torso (upper body), short arms and legs, and a large head. Dwarfs look different from both regular-sized people and midgets because their bodies are not normally proportioned.

What's the difference between a dwarf and a midget?

A midget's whole body is small but normally proportioned. Some midgets are no taller than a five-year-old.

Will a dwarf ever grow to normal size?

No, a dwarf will never grow to a normal adult size.

How long does it take to find out if you are a dwarf?

Doctors can usually tell at birth that an infant will be a dwarf by its large head. Dwarfs may also have a dip in the top of their nose and a differently shaped jaw.

Does being a dwarf affect your intelligence?

Being a dwarf does not affect your mind. A dwarf is as intelligent as anyone—or even smarter, like our friend Amy!

How do you become a dwarf?

You are born a dwarf. It is an inherited trait, like eye color or skin color. Anyone can have a child who is a dwarf. The chance of two regular-sized people having a dwarf is one in 40,000. If a family has one dwarf child, their chance of having another child who is a also dwarf is again one in 40,000.

Can a dwarf have children of normal size?

If a dwarf is married to a person of normal size, there is a 50 percent chance that their child will be a dwarf. But if a dwarf is married to another dwarf, there is a 75 percent chance that the couple's child will be a dwarf. If a dwarf couple has a regular-sized child, that child will not carry the gene for dwarfism.

What kind of physical problems do dwarfs have?

Dwarfs have to watch their weight because extra pounds can cause stress on the joints in their legs. Amy has some problems with her hips and her back that make her unable to carry heavy things. Because their arms and legs are so short, dwarfs have trouble reaching things that regular-sized people have no trouble with, such as the faucets on a sink or the light switch near a door. Another problem for dwarfs is getting in and out of places.

Anthony Allen

Amy practices her clarinet 15 to 20 hours every week

Do dwarfs have to go to a special store to buy clothes?
Dwarfs usually buy regular clothes from any store and then shorten the arms and legs.

What is Little People of America?
Little People of America (LPA) is a big organization that helps dwarfs and their families. All the people who belong to the organization support and help each other out. Once a year, the LPA holds a national convention where families can meet other people in similar situations from all over the nation. At the confer-

ence the LPA educates people about new things to make life easier for dwarfs and their families. It also tells them about doctors who are working to help dwarfs.

Our Poem Dedicated to Amy

> *Amy may be small,*
> *But that doesn't matter at all.*
> *The clarinet she loves to play,*
> *In the symphony we will see her*
> * someday.*

OUR VISION FOR A BETTER TOMORROW

Some people believe that when they become a friend to someone who has a disability, they are doing that person a favor. We know that people are really doing *themselves* a favor. There is so much to learn from those who have had experiences different from our own. We want to share what we have learned through making new friends.

Shawn Lewis is just a kid who wants to be treated like one of the guys. He has taught us not to give up our dreams, even when they seem impossible. Most of all, Shawn has shown us the greatest gift in life you can have is the unselfish love of others. Because of his family's example, we all will become more involved in other people's lives.

 Mikelle Learned is not able to talk, but she shared her positive attitude with us in other ways. If we can have the same attitude, it will make the world a better place. She let us know, in her own way, that we should think about what we *can* do. She challenged us to look for the way around roadblocks because nothing is impossible if you really try.

 Nathan Moutray showed us the importance of never giving up. Even when school is difficult, keep trying because your teachers and parents will help you get through. Learning is not the same for everyone, and we have learned the most important thing is to find the way that is best for you.

 Lisa Ferrerio just loves life and she shows this in many ways. We know that because of her determination and drive, she will do great things. She taught us that love and friendship, like the kind her family and her dog Kosmo give her, matter much more than physical things. But most of all, Lisa wanted us to re-member, "Look at what I can do, not at what I can't."

 Lance Petrillo and his family had to deal with a problem for many years, and they didn't even know what it was. The Petrillos taught us not to give up and to keep looking for help when you think something isn't right. They also encouraged us to look for strength in your family and friends. They will get you through the hard times.

 David Billars doesn't worry about the big problems in the world. He taught us not to judge people by how they look but to get to know them by their actions. He likes people who are kind and willing to lend a helping hand. David has shown us the beauty of true friendship, loyalty, and laughter.

 Kelly Young understands that each day in life is special. He doesn't think about what might have been, he enjoys what is. He showed us that there are not many differences between us, and giving it all you've got is what counts.

 Gena Perry displayed a lot of courage as she was telling her story to us. Although she sounds a little different from hearing people, her message came through loud and clear. Don't turn away from someone just because they may not be the same as you. Gena taught us that listening doesn't always have to come from your ears. It can also come from your heart.

 Joe Kovach has taught us always to look forward to tomorrow. He made us stop and think about our own skills and how we should look at life in a different way. He showed us how he never lets anything stand in his way. From Joe we learned never to stop trying to see the good in our lives, no matter what happens.

 Amy Allen's sense of humor and laughter make the world more joyful. She taught us to look at ourselves and to be happy with who we are. Your size doesn't matter, it's what's inside that is important. And always keep a song in your heart.

Our new friends showed us that we should not judge people before we get to know them. If we look for the best in each person, we will all become better people. We know the world will be a better place if we all look for the gifts in the people we meet.

WESTRIDGE YOUNG WRITERS
WORKSHOP PARTICIPANTS

Director: Judith H. Cozzens
Assistant Director: Roxanne Carlson Boat

Mrs. Evan's fifth grade class

AUTHORS AND TEACHERS

Mrs. Cherylene Evan's fifth grade class wrote about Shawn Lewis

Nick Adamo
Andra Nicole Arnold
Dominic Atencio
Brett Bell
Christopher Lee Burch
Marella Canfield-Jones
Emily Devliegher
Seth Eaton
Alan Hawkins

Matt Heye
Chris Husted
Jill Kotala
Nicole Kramer
Bryson Maes
Dustin Morrow
Jennifer Muller
Micah Schmid
Leanda Shackelford
Courtney Ward
Micah Weinberg
Chad Williams
Matt Worland
Tommy Wrzesinski
Kristen York
Charles Youssef

Lori Stober

Mrs. Herald's fifth grade class

Mrs. Marsha Herald's fifth grade class wrote about Mikelle Learned

Zachary Arnone
Jamie Brantley
Gary Connell
Amy Cooper
James Dykes
Matthew Farnum
Ashleigh Ferris
Joshua Funderburg
Matthew Gallegos
Kathryn Good
Amy Jessop

Hope Kamlay
Justin Krista
Eric Miliauskas
Jacob Montoya
Donald Moore
Justin Murff
Amy Pomranka
James Porter
Elizabeth Powis
Brandon Rachetts
Brandon Ramirez
Laura Swigert
Alyssa Toland
Angela Wegher
Randia Weinberg

Mrs. Donna Burris' fourth grade class wrote about Nathan Moutray

Mrs. Burris' fourth grade class

Mark Dickson

Adam Acree
Danielle Alcon
Joe Anciaux
Ryan Arbogast
Donald Arnold
Sam Bader
Chris Ball
Dyllan Beck
Teb Beran
Travis Book
Scott Chikuma
Zach Collins
Jacque Fowler
Adell Gallagher
Jeremy Gutierrez
Jack Guzlow
Jesse Hansen
Elicia Hays
Alisha Hernlund
Alex Hindman
Nathan Hosey
Sara Lane
Ryan Logan
Nick Manning
Austin Meinen
Joe Miller
Tarra Needham
Pornchai Pannotayan
Katy Sears
Lindsay Snyder
Katie Strade
Gwen Tewksbury
Joey Trounce
Vanessa Valentine
Mark Vangundy

Diane Holstein

Mrs. Seidel's and Mrs. O'Lear's sixth grade class

Mrs. Judy Seidel's and Mrs. Stacey O'Lear's sixth grade class wrote about Lisa Ferrerio

Natacha Almaquer
Gina Beller
Timisha Buskey
Joaquin Castro
Doug Gaumintz
Karen Hashman
Jennifer Jay
Eric Lindgren
Justin MacLeod
Marissa Martinez
Jerome McClain

Heather Miller
Tony Monaco
Carrie Mondragon
Pat Murphy
Rene Ortega
Matt Reed
Ricci Roth
Jarrod Ruckle
Jennifer Schuler
Kristen Searey
Amber Thompson
Macario Vigil
Mike Wilson
Matt Workman
Kyle Yushka

Mark Dickson

Miss Wabler's fifth grade class

Miss Theresa Wabler's fifth grade class wrote about Lance Petrillo

Travis Beach
Bobby Beck
Jeff Bissonnette
Kirsten Carson
Dustin Dewitt
Isaac Ray Edwards
Kevin Everson
Nancee Feagans
Wade Fletcher
Jerome Foss
Judy Funk
Jamie Lester
Cameron Magner
Brian Marsh
Lance Petrillo
Kendra Phelan
Alexi Rothschild
Jason Schoshke
Camille Schroeder
Stefanie Southall
Erika Sullivan
Shannon Thacker
Jackie M. Tighe
Cody Wallace
Brandon Weaver
Nicole Wessels

Mark Dickson

Mrs. Caplan's fifth grade class and David's Circle of Friends

Mrs. Arna B. Caplan's fifth grade class wrote about David Billars

Amber Alley
John Anderson
Bri Biddle
Jacob Daniel Brecht
Joshua J. Burroughs
Kacey Chamberlain
Erik Michael Chik
Justin William Crane
Beau Daniel Duncan
Carrie Fann
Eric Fogleman

Noah Griego
Valerie Haile
Katie Mary Kern
Aaron Christopher Martinez
Melissa Sue Medrano
Keri Pokorny
Michelle Lynn Powis
Chris Rains
Jason Paul Romaniec
Paul Michael Ruzzo
Melody Schoenberger
Jeremy Tyler Skadsen
Jonathan Allen Tidd
Troy Curtis Ward

John Twohig

Mrs. Healy's fourth grade class

Mrs. Helen Healy's fourth grade class wrote about Kelly Young

Aimee Brown
Lee Clintsman Jr.
Nikolai Dobbs
Jeff Hirsch
Catherine Hurd
Chris Jungmann
Douglas Klutzke
Lisa Lyttle
Joe Michalitsch
Nicole Miller
Mike Murray
Larry Joe Nava
Chad Nelson
Erin Netzloff

Brenda O'Neill
Jenny Perry
Richie Pierce
Jennifer Roehl
Nicole Ryder
Randy Sandhofer
Kevin Scarrella
Jeff Shaffer
Lynnette Tschida
Ashley Twardowski
Julie Vanek
Katie Vogt
Jeremy Wegleitner
Lindsey Williams
Jenny Zielinksi

Christie Logsdon

Mrs. Avery's third/fourth grade class

Mrs. Barbara Avery's third/ fourth grade class wrote about Gena Perry

David Baldwin
Jonathan Dale
Gregory Dunn
Derek Patterson
Preston Vincent
Michael Yager
Matthew Bell
Eric Crouch
Mike Dyck

Katie Combs
Leigh Ann Dale
Kelly Eggers
Katie Jenkins
Carrie Ann Koppernolle
Laurien White
Jessica Wright
Amanda Buschbach
Chelsea M. Koch
Michaela Perry
Stacey Schenider
Morgan Scott
Kristen Spink
Stacy Whitton

Anthony Allen

Mrs. Barker's fifth grade class

Mrs. Karen S. Barker's fifth grade class wrote about Joe Kovach and Amy Allen

Jaime L. Allison
Adriann Baker
Katie R. Baker
Shelly Lynn Ball
Dave A. Bigley
Jaime L. Guthrie
Nichole I. Cox
Bryan C. Dankert
Jacee Elbeck
Matthew C. Feeney
Brandon M. George

Jon D. Geypens
Zach J. Haberler
Chris M. Jersild
Briana Kass
Aaron Michael Kirgan
Jessica R. LeMaster
Pat Nedele
Jackie Pilling
Shaz D. Sedighzadeh
Megan E. Stenbeck
James Freedon Tomasi
Eric Towner
Christopher J. Voelker
Tessa Jean Wiederspahn

CONTRIBUTORS AND SPEAKERS

Thanks to all the experts and volunteers who shared their time and knowledge with us:

Dr. Samuel Baron
John Carlton Boat
Jean Cable
Dr. Jim Cullen
Susan Dareau
Marian Ernst
Linda Gray
Ralph Hancock
Debbie Hauserman
Ron Horn
Faith Keys
Marge Knell
Craig Knippenberg
Lonnie Kocsis
John Leslie
Karen Litz
Cathy Madigan
Donna Massine
Zora Milne
Pamela Murray
Dr. Carol Nichols
Jo Lynn Osborne
Lisa Patterson
Goldie Pizel
Amy Pound
Pam Wachter
Cora Woogen

INDEX

THE KIDS EXPLORE SERIES

Written By Kids For Kids

Written by elementary school students in the Westridge Young Writers Workshop in Littleton, Colorado, the Kids Explore series celebrates the wonderful diversity of American culture.

KIDS EXPLORE America's African-American Heritage

ISBN 1-56261-090-2

". . . [T]his special book will outlive Black History Month, and kids and grown-ups, too, will find this enjoyable reading all year round."

—*L.A. Parent*

KIDS EXPLORE America's Hispanic Heritage

ISBN 1-56261-034-1

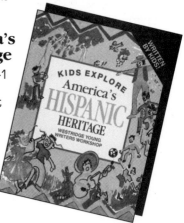

"An enthusiastic and genuine glimpse into the Hispanic culture that is part of our national heritage. Chapters on history, food, stories, jokes, and biographical entries give information in a low-key, informative, and readable manner."

—*School Library Journal*

KIDS EXPLORE America's Japanese-American Heritage

ISBN 1-56261-155-0

This kids'-eye view of Japanese-American culture includes history, heroes and heroines, an exploration of food, fun, celebrations, and games, contributions to art, poetry, and the martial arts, as well as a list of Japanese words and what they mean.

KIDS EXPLORE the Gifts of Children with Special Needs

ISBN 1-56261-156-9

This book is a sensitive and thought-provoking look at the gifts of children with special needs as seen by their peers. They tell us the stories of ten courageous individuals with disabilities that include dyslexia, attention deficit disorder, cerebral palsy, hemophilia, blindness, and hearing impairment.